Slow Cooker & Family Recipes

Blueberry Hill

Slow Cooker & Family Recipes

This edition published in 2013
LOVE FOOD is an imprint of Parragon Books Ltd

Parragon
Chartist House
15–17 Trim Street
Bath, BA1 1HA, UK

ISBN: 978-1-78186-742-6

Printed in China

Notes for the Reader

This book uses both metric and imperial measurements. Follow the same
units of measurement throughout; do not mix metric and imperial. All
spoon measurements are level: teaspoons are assumed to be 5 ml, and
tablespoons are assumed to be 15 ml. Unless otherwise stated, milk is
assumed to be full fat, eggs and individual vegetables are medium, and
pepper is freshly ground black pepper. Unless otherwise stated, all root
vegetables should be washed in plain water and peeled prior to using.

For best results, use a food thermometer when cooking meat and
poultry – check the latest government guidelines for current advice.

Garnishes, decorations and serving suggestions are all optional and not
necessarily included in the recipe ingredients or method.

The times given are an approximate guide only. Preparation times differ
according to the techniques used by different people and the cooking
times may also vary from those given. Optional ingredients, variations
or serving suggestions have not been included in the time calculations.

Recipes using raw or very lightly cooked eggs should be avoided by
infants, the elderly, pregnant women, convalescents and anyone suffering
from an illness. Pregnant and breastfeeding women are advised to avoid
eating peanuts and peanut products. Sufferers from nut allergies should
be aware that some of the ready-made ingredients used in the recipes in
this book may contain nuts. Always check the packaging before use.

Contents

1 ❀ Starters & Snacks 12

2 ❀ Slow Cooker Favourites 50

3 ❀ Salads & Side Dishes 126

4 ❀ Something Sweet 184

Welcome to

Blueberry Hill

H ere at Blueberry Hill we understand that busy families
need easy and simple solutions. No one has the time
to spend hours over a hot cooker when the children
need to be picked up from school, there's a deadline to hit
at work and you need to conjure up something from the
leftovers in the refrigerator. The good news is that with our
recipes you can still feed your family good, honest, wholesome
and nutritious meals but you won't feel like you are tied to
your kitchen!

Our books are designed to introduce (or re-introduce) you to
healthy, economical and delicious food. Many of the recipes
are lovingly remembered classics, while others feature
familiar ingredients prepared from a fresh perspective.

Blueberry Hill books are produced by a consortium of
top-notch cooks and food professionals who have created
a collection of hundreds of delectable family-style recipes,
from starters to desserts. Each and every dish has been
carefully tested, assuring perfect results every time.

Whether you consider yourself a gourmet or a novice cook we're sure that our books will soon become a well-used collection on your shelf. In *Slow Cooker & Family Recipes*, you'll find a diverse and delicious range of 130 recipes. We've put together our favourite dishes, from classics such as *Traditional Pot Roast* and *Chicken Stew* to more exotic recipes such as *Sea Bass in Lemon Sauce*. In addition to the main dishes, you'll find a selection of starters and snacks, and dozens of salads and side dishes.

So what's more to say than here's to enjoying less time in the kitchen and more time with the family.

Happy cooking and warmest wishes from all of us at *Blueberry Hill*.

Storecupboard Essentials

A well stocked storecupboard helps make life a little easier when trying to plan out what to cook. The ingredients listed below are the things you'll regularly find on our shopping list.

Dry ingredients

Pasta Spaghetti and macaroni are good basic pastas but for a broader choice add lasagne sheets, cannelloni tubes, fusilli, farfalle, tagliatelle and conchiglie.

Rice Every cupboard should have a good long-grain rice such as basmati rice, supplemented with risotto rice and brown rice.

Noodles Most noodles are associated with south-east Asian cooking. Make sure you have both egg noodles and rice noodles for use in soups and stir-fries.

Flour Plain flour works beautifully for thickening casseroles, making sauces and coating food before cooking. Self-raising flour is often used for baking, while bread making generally requires specific strong flour due to higher gluten levels.

Sugar Granulated and caster sugar and soft brown sugar cover most of the basic needs, but some recipes will call for icing sugar for making icings and decoration.

Nuts and seeds Walnuts, almonds, pine nuts and cashews can be used to add extra crunch and texture to savoury dishes and baked goods. Make sure to store them in airtight containers. Sesame seeds are useful for many Asian-inspired dishes.

Oils & vinegars

Extra virgin olive oil Ideal for drizzling over salads, extra virgin olive oil is produced from the first cold-pressing of the olives and is a premium olive oil with a peppery, fruity flavour.

Vegetable oil Made of a blend of various oils, this is best used for frying as it is very greasy.

Groundnut oil Suitable for drizzling, dressings and mayonnaise as well as forms of cooking, this is a very versatile oil.

Wine vinegars Available in many different varieties, mainly red, white and sherry. They can be used for dressings, marinades and sauces or sprinkled over foods.

Balsamic vinegar This delicious vinegar is thick, dark and slightly sweet. It is made from grape juice that is aged in barrels over a number of years.

Herbs & spices

If you don't have fresh ones, it's always good to have dried herbs and spices to hand.

Chilli powder This powdered mixture includes dried chillies, cumin, coriander and cloves. Use it to flavour soups and stews.

Paprika This spice is made from ground sweet red pepper pods and its flavour can vary from mild, sweet and pungent to fiery hot. It is excellent in salads and as a garnish.

Ginger Dried ginger is particularly good with fruit, biscuits and condiments.

Bay leaves Dried bay leaves add a good pungent flavour to soups, sauces and casseroles. They are usually discarded once the food has absorbed their flavour.

Old Bay seasoning Look for this blend of seasonings at speciality shops, or make it by grinding 6 bay leaves, 4 whole cloves, 1 tablespoon each of celery seeds, whole black peppercorns and sweet paprika, ½ teaspoon of whole cardamom seeds and ¼ teaspoon of mace in a spice grinder.

Chives Relatives of the onion family, these herbs can be added to salads, soups, cream cheese and egg dishes.

Garlic Fresh cloves of garlic store well or you can buy jars of chopped garlic preserved in oil or dried garlic.

Thyme A versatile herb that is good with meat, poultry, egg and potato dishes. Use in soups, sauces, roasts, bakes and stews.

Five-spice Chinese five-spice powder is a blend of cloves, cinnamon, fennel seeds, Szechuan peppercorns and star anise. It is very popular in stir-fries.

Mixed spice This spice blend includes cinnamon, cloves, mace, nutmeg, coriander and allspice. Its warm flavour is delicious in fruit dishes, bread, cakes, biscuits and pies.

Other items

Stock cubes Great for use in casseroles and soups if you do not have time to make or buy fresh stock.

Tomato purée This condensed purée adds a more intense flavour to sauces and soups.

Canned tomatoes Always useful for a variety of dishes, from sauces and soups to stews and casseroles.

Canned beans Always have a few cans of beans to hand, from red kidney beans to lentils and chickpeas. They don't require soaking and can be very useful.

Canned fish Many dishes can use canned or fresh fish. Tuna, crab and anchovies are all useful for salads or pasta dishes.

Pickled foods Pickles, pickled onions and capers make perfect accompaniments and garnishes for meat and vegetable dishes.

Olives It's always useful to have a can or a bottle of olives in the cupboard. They are delicious in salads, pastas and on pizzas and can be blended to make dips.

Soy sauce A popular Chinese sauce, soy sauce is used in all south-east Asian foods and adds a salty flavour. Soy comes in light and dark varieties: use the light one with shellfish and the dark one with duck and meat.

Worcestershire sauce This strongly flavoured sauce adds a spicy kick to casseroles and soups.

Starters & Snacks

Prawn Cocktail

900 g/2 lb king prawns, deveined but unpeeled

Lemon wedges, to serve

For the poaching liquid

2.8 litres/5 pints cold water

½ onion, sliced

2 garlic cloves, peeled and bruised

2 sprigs tarragon

1 bay leaf

1 tbsp Old Bay seasoning (see page 10)

juice of ½ lemon

1 tsp black peppercorns

For the cocktail sauce

125 ml/4 fl oz tomato ketchup

4 tbsp chilli sauce

4 tbsp horseradish sauce, or to taste

1 tsp lemon juice

1 tsp Worcestershire sauce

Dash of hot pepper sauce (optional)

Pinch of salt

For the sauce, combine all ingredients in a small bowl, mix thoroughly and refrigerate for at least 1 hour before serving.

Prawn shells add flavour to the poaching liquid. If you can't find prawns with the shell on and deveined – where the intestinal track is removed – get shell-on prawns and use a pair of scissors to make a cut through the shell, down the back of the prawns. Then use a small sharp knife to make a 3 mm/⅛ inch deep incision and remove the intestinal track. Rinse under cold water.

Add all the poaching liquid ingredients to a large saucepan. Place over a high heat and bring to a simmer. Turn the heat down to low and simmer for 30 minutes.

Fill a mixing bowl with iced water and set aside. Turn the heat under the poaching liquid to high and bring to the boil. Add the prawns and boil for 5 minutes or until cooked through. Using a slotted spoon, remove the prawns from the poaching liquid and transfer to the bowl of iced water.

When the prawns are cold, drain well. The prawns can be served with the shells on, or peel the shells off and arrange the prawns around the rim of a cocktail glass. Serve with the cocktail sauce and lemon wedges.

Maryland Crab Cakes

1 egg, beaten

2 tbsp mayonnaise

½ tsp Dijon mustard

¼ tsp Worcestershire sauce

½ tsp Old Bay seasoning (see page 10)

¼ tsp salt

Pinch of cayenne pepper

10 cream crackers

450 g/1 lb fresh lump crabmeat, well drained

85 g/3 oz fresh breadcrumbs

1 tbsp vegetable oil

25 g/1 oz unsalted butter

For the tartare sauce

225 g/8 oz mayonnaise

4 tbsp sweet gerkin relish

1 tbsp finely chopped onion

1 tbsp chopped capers

1 tbsp chopped parsley

1½ tbsp lemon juice

Dash of Worcestershire sauce

Few drops of hot pepper sauce

Salt and pepper

Whisk together the egg, mayonnaise, mustard, Worcestershire sauce, Old Bay seasoning, salt and cayenne pepper in a mixing bowl. Crush the crackers into very fine crumbs and add to the bowl. Stir until combined. Leave to stand for 5 minutes.

Gently fold in the crabmeat. Cover the bowl and refrigerate for at least 1 hour.

Meanwhile, for the tartare sauce, mix together all the ingredients in a bowl. Refrigerate at least 1 hour before serving.

Sprinkle the breadcrumbs lightly over a large plate. Shape the crab mixture into 6 cakes and place on the plate. Dust the top of each crab cake lightly with the breadcrumbs. These cakes are almost all crab, which makes them fragile. They will bind together as the egg cooks and a golden-brown crust forms.

Heat the vegetable oil and butter in a large frying pan over a medium–high heat. When the foam from the butter begins to dissipate, carefully transfer each crab cake to the pan. Sauté for about 4 minutes each side until golden brown. Drain on kitchen paper and serve with the tartare sauce.

Vegetarian Spring Rolls

55 g/2 oz fine thread noodles

2 tbsp groundnut oil, plus extra for deep-frying

2 garlic cloves, crushed

½ tsp grated fresh ginger

40 g/1½ oz oyster mushrooms, thinly sliced

2 spring onions, finely chopped

50 g/1¾ oz beansprouts

1 small carrot, finely grated

½ tsp sesame oil

1 tbsp light soy sauce

1 tbsp rice wine or dry sherry

¼ tsp ground pepper

1 tbsp chopped fresh coriander

1 tbsp chopped fresh mint

24 spring roll wrappers

½ tsp cornflour

1 tbsp water

Place the noodles in a heatproof bowl, pour over enough boiling water to cover and leave to stand for 4 minutes. Drain, rinse in cold water, then drain again. Cut into 5-cm/2-inch lengths.

Heat the 2 tablespoons of groundnut oil in a wok or wide saucepan over a high heat. Add the garlic, ginger, mushrooms, spring onions, beansprouts and carrot and stir-fry for about 1 minute until just soft.

Stir in the sesame oil, soy sauce, rice wine, pepper, coriander and mint, then remove from the heat. Stir in the rice noodles.

Arrange the spring roll wrappers on a work surface, pointing diagonally. Mix the cornflour with the water. Brush the edges of a wrapper with a little of the cornflour mixture. Spoon a little filling onto a pointed side of the wrapper.

Roll the point of the wrapper over the filling, then fold the side points inwards over the filling. Continue to roll up the wrapper away from you, moistening the tip with more cornflour mixture to secure the roll. Repeat until all the filling and wrappers have been used.

Heat enough oil for deep-frying in a wok or deep pan to 180–190°C/350–375°F or until a cube of bread browns in 30 seconds. Add rolls, in batches, and deep-fry for 2–3 minutes each until golden brown and crisp. Serve hot.

Sweet & Sour Chicken Wings

serves 4-6

550 g/1 lb 4 oz chicken wings, tips removed

2 celery sticks, chopped

750 ml/1¼ pints boiling chicken stock

2 tbsp cornflour

3 tbsp white wine vinegar or rice vinegar

3 tbsp dark soy sauce

5 tbsp sweet chilli sauce

4 tbsp soft brown sugar

400 g/14 oz canned pineapple chunks in juice, drained

125 g/4½ oz bamboo shoots

½ green pepper, deseeded and thinly sliced

½ red pepper, deseeded and thinly sliced

Salt

Put the chicken wings and celery in the slow cooker and season with salt. Pour in the stock, cover and cook on low for 5 hours or until the chicken is tender and the juices run clear when a skewer is inserted into the thickest part of the meat.

Drain the chicken wings, reserving 350 ml/12 fl oz of the stock, and keep warm. Pour the reserved stock into a saucepan and stir in the cornflour. Add the vinegar, soy sauce and chilli sauce. Place over a medium heat and stir in the sugar. Cook, stirring constantly, for 5 minutes or until the sugar has dissolved completely and the sauce is thickened and smooth.

Reduce the heat, stir in the pineapple, bamboo shoots and green and red peppers and simmer gently for 2–3 minutes. Stir in the chicken wings until they are thoroughly coated, then transfer to a serving platter.

Lamb & Rice Soup

serves 6

1 kg/2 lb 4 oz boned leg of lamb, cut into 2.5-cm/1-inch pieces

2 lamb bones, cracked

3 garlic cloves, peeled

2 litres/3½ pints water

85 g/3 oz basmati rice

6 slices French bread

2 tbsp chopped fresh parsley

Salt and pepper

Put the lamb, lamb bones and garlic cloves into a large saucepan and pour in the water. Season well with salt and pepper and bring to the boil, skimming off any foam that rises to the surface. Transfer the mixture to the slow cooker, cover and cook on low for 5 hours.

Meanwhile, soak the rice in several changes of cold water for 30 minutes, then drain.

Remove and discard the lamb bones and garlic cloves from the slow cooker, then stir in the rice. Re-cover and cook on low for a further 2–2½ hours until the lamb and rice are tender.

Shortly before serving, preheat the grill. Place the bread slices on the grill rack and lightly grill on both sides. Put a piece of bread into each individual serving bowl. Ladle the soup over the bread, sprinkle with the parsley and serve immediately.

Steak & Mozzarella Sandwiches

serves 4

1 French baguette

350 g/12 oz boneless fillet steak

3 tbsp olive oil

1 onion, thinly sliced

1 green pepper, deseeded and thinly sliced

55 g/2 oz fresh buffalo mozzarella, thinly sliced

Salt and pepper

Hot pepper sauce, to serve

Cut the baguette into 4 equal lengths, then cut each piece in half horizontally. Thinly slice the steak across its grain.

Heat 2 tablespoons of the oil in a large frying pan over a medium heat, add the onion and green pepper and cook, stirring occasionally, for 10–15 minutes until both vegetables are softened and the onion is golden brown. Push the mixture to one side of the frying pan

Heat the remaining oil in the frying pan over a medium heat. When hot, add the steak and stir-fry for 4–5 minutes until tender. Stir the onion mixture and steak together and season with salt and pepper.

Preheat the grill to medium. Divide the steak mixture between the 4 bottom halves of bread and top with the cheese. Place them on a grill rack and grill for 1–2 minutes until the cheese has melted, then cover with the top halves of bread and press down gently. Serve immediately with the hot pepper sauce.

Hummus with Crudités

serves 4

250 g/9 oz canned chickpeas, drained and rinsed

4 tbsp tahini

2 garlic cloves

125 ml/4 fl oz lemon juice

2–3 tbsp water

1 tbsp olive oil

1 tbsp chopped fresh parsley

Pinch of cayenne pepper

Salt and pepper

For the crudités

4 carrots

4 celery sticks

½ small cauliflower

1 green pepper, deseeded

1 red pepper, deseeded

8 radishes

For the crudités, cut the carrots and celery into thin batons, cut the cauliflower into small florets and cut the green and red peppers into thin strips.

Place the chickpeas, tahini, garlic and lemon juice in a blender or food processor and season with salt and pepper to taste.

Process the ingredients, gradually adding water to the mixture as necessary, until the consistency becomes smooth and creamy. Taste and adjust the seasoning if necessary.

Transfer the mixture into a serving bowl and make a hollow in the centre with the back of a spoon. Pour the olive oil into the hollow, then sprinkle the hummus with the chopped parsley and cayenne pepper.

Arrange the prepared crudités on a large serving platter and serve immediately with the hummus.

Clams with Bacon & Breadcrumb Topping

serves 6

25 g/1 oz unsalted butter

3 streaky bacon rashers, each sliced into 6 pieces

3 tbsp finely diced red pepper

3 garlic cloves, finely chopped

25 g/1 oz dried breadcrumbs

1 tbsp of finely grated Parmesan

Pinch of pepper

Pinch of salt

18 medium-sized (about 6 cm/2½ inches) live clams, scrubbed

2 tbsp chopped fresh flat-leaf parsley

Rock salt and lemon wedges, to serve

Heat the butter in a frying pan over a medium heat. Add the bacon and sauté until cooked but not quite crisp. Using a slotted spoon, transfer the bacon to a plate and reserve.

Add the red pepper to the bacon dripping in the frying pan and cook for 2 minutes. Add the garlic and cook for 1 minute more. Turn off the heat and stir in the breadcrumbs, Parmesan, pepper and salt. Reserve the mixture until needed.

Discard any clams with broken shells and any that refuse to close when tapped. Pour about 5 cm/2 inches of water into a large saucepan with a tight-fitting lid and bring to a rapid boil over a high heat. Add the clams, cover and cook for about 5 minutes or just until the shells open. It's critical to remove and drain the clams as soon as they open. Allow the clams to cool until they can be handled.

Preheat the grill to high. Discard any clams that remain closed. Twist and pull the clam shells apart and remove the clam. Place the clam back into the deeper of the 2 shell halves. Spread the rock salt on a heatproof baking dish and set the clams on top of the salt, pressing in slightly.

Divide the breadcrumb mixture between the clam shells and top each with a piece of bacon. Cook under the preheated grill until the tops are browned and the edges of the bacon are crisp. Sprinkle over the fresh parsley and serve hot with lemon wedges.

Yorkshire Puddings

makes 6

2 tbsp beef dripping or
vegetable fat
125 g/4½ oz plain flour
½ tsp salt
2 large eggs
225 ml/8 fl oz milk

Preheat the oven to 220°C/425°F/Gas Mark 7.

Grease 6 metal Yorkshire pudding moulds or 6 holes in
a bun tin with the dripping or vegetable fat. Place into the
preheated oven while you make the batter.

Sift the flour and salt together into a large mixing bowl
and make a well in the centre. Break the eggs into the
well, add the milk and beat, gradually drawing in the flour
from the side, to make a smooth batter. Remove the
moulds from the oven and spoon in the batter until they
are about half-full.

Bake in the preheated oven for 20–25 minutes, without
opening the door, until the puddings are well risen, puffed
and golden brown. Serve immediately.

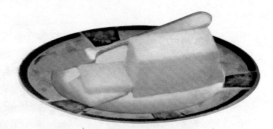

Sweet Potato Cakes

450 g/1 lb sweet potatoes

2 garlic cloves, crushed

1 small fresh green chilli, chopped

2 fresh coriander sprigs, chopped

1 tbsp dark soy sauce

Plain flour, for shaping

Vegetable oil, for frying

Sesame seeds, for sprinkling

For the soy-tomato sauce

2 tsp vegetable oil

1 garlic clove, finely chopped

1½ tsp finely chopped fresh ginger

3 tomatoes, peeled and chopped

2 tbsp dark soy sauce

1 tbsp lime juice

2 tbsp chopped fresh coriander

To make the soy-tomato sauce, heat the oil in a wok and stir-fry the garlic and ginger for about 1 minute. Add the tomatoes and stir-fry for a further 2 minutes. Remove from the heat and stir in the soy sauce, lime juice and chopped coriander. Set aside and keep warm.

Peel the sweet potatoes and grate finely (you can do this with a food processor). Place the garlic, chilli and coriander in a mortar and crush to a smooth paste with a pestle. Stir in the soy sauce and mix with the sweet potatoes.

Divide the mixture into 12 equal-sized portions. Dip into flour and pat into a flat, round disc shape.

Heat a shallow layer of oil in a wide frying pan. Cook the sweet potato cakes in batches over a high heat until golden, turning once.

Drain on kitchen paper and sprinkle with the sesame seeds. Serve hot with the soy-tomato sauce.

Onion & Mozzarella Tartlets

makes 4

250 g/9 oz ready-made puff pastry, thawed, if frozen

2 red onions

1 red pepper

8 cherry tomatoes, halved

115 g/4 oz mozzarella cheese, grated

6–8 fresh thyme sprigs

Roll out the pastry to make 4 x 7.5-cm/3-inch squares. Using a sharp knife, trim the edges of the pastry, reserving the trimmings. Let the pastry chill in the refrigerator for 30 minutes.

Place the pastry squares on a baking tray. Brush a little water along each edge of the pastry squares and use the reserved pastry trimmings to make a rim around each tartlet.

Preheat the grill. Cut the red onions into thin wedges and halve and deseed the red pepper. Place the onions and red pepper in a roasting tin. Cook under the preheated grill for 15 minutes or until charred.

Preheat the oven to 200°C/400°F/Gas Mark 6. Place the grilled pepper halves in a plastic bag and leave to sweat for 10 minutes. Peel off the skin from the peppers and cut the flesh into strips.

Line the pastry squares with squares of foil. Bake in the preheated oven for 10 minutes.

Remove the foil from the pastry squares, then divide the onions, pepper strips, tomatoes and cheese between them and sprinkle with the fresh thyme. Return to the oven for 15 minutes or until the pastry is golden. Serve hot.

Crispy Chicken Goujons with Honey & Mustard Dip

serves 8

125 g/4½ oz plain flour

2 tsp salt

1 tsp garlic salt

1 tsp chipotle pepper

½ tsp white pepper

4 large skinless, boneless chicken breasts, cut into 1-cm/ ½-inch strips

4 eggs, beaten

1 tbsp milk

200 g/7 oz Japanese-style panko breadcrumbs

Vegetable oil, for frying

For the honey & mustard dip

115 g/4 oz mayonnaise

2 tbsp Dijon mustard

2 tbsp yellow mustard

1 tbsp rice vinegar

2 tbsp clear honey

½ tsp hot pepper sauce (optional)

Combine the flour, salt, garlic salt, chipotle and white pepper in a large, sealable plastic bag. Shake to mix. Add the chicken strips, seal the bag and shake vigorously to coat evenly.

In a mixing bowl, whisk together the eggs and milk. Add the chicken strips, shaking off the excess flour as you remove them from the bag. Stir until the strips are completely coated in the egg mixture.

Pour the breadcrumbs in a shallow dish. Use one hand to remove the chicken strips from the bowl of eggs, a few at a time, allowing the excess egg to drip off, and place in the dish of breadcrumbs. Use the other hand to coat the chicken in the breadcrumbs, pressing them in firmly. As they are breaded, place the strips on a plate. Leave the chicken strips to rest for 10–15 minutes before frying.

Pour about 1 cm/½ inch of oil in a large, heavy-based frying pan (ideally cast iron) and set over a medium–high heat to 180–190°C/350–375°F or until a cube of bread browns within 30 seconds. Cook the chicken strips, in batches, for 2–3 minutes per side or until golden brown and cooked through. Drain on kitchen paper and keep in a warm oven until all the chicken strips have been fried.

To make the honey and mustard dip, combine all the ingredients and mix well. Serve immediately with the chicken goujons.

Tomato & Lentil Soup

serves 4

2 tbsp vegetable oil

1 onion, chopped

1 garlic clove, finely chopped

2 celery sticks, chopped

2 carrots, chopped

1 tsp ground cumin

1 tsp ground coriander

140 g/5 oz canned red or yellow lentils, rinsed

1 tbsp tomato purée

1.2 litres/2 pints vegetable stock

400 g/14 oz canned chopped tomatoes

1 bay leaf

Salt and pepper

Soured cream and toasted crusty bread, to serve

Heat the oil in a saucepan. Add the onion and garlic and cook over low heat, stirring occasionally, for 5 minutes until softened. Stir in the celery and carrots and cook for a further 4 minutes. Stir in the cumin and coriander and cook, stirring, for 1 minute, then add the lentils.

Mix the tomato purée with a little of the stock in a small bowl and add to the pan with the remaining stock, the tomatoes and bay leaf. Bring to the boil, then transfer to the slow cooker. Stir well, cover and cook on low for 3½–4 hours.

Remove and discard the bay leaf. Transfer the soup to a food processor or blender and process until smooth. Season to taste with salt and pepper. Ladle into warmed soup bowls, top each with a swirl of soured cream and serve immediately with toasted crusty bread.

Deep-fried Chilli Corn Balls

serves 4

6 spring onions, sliced

3 tbsp chopped fresh coriander

175 g/6 oz canned sweetcorn kernels

1 tsp mild chilli powder

1 tbsp sweet chilli sauce, plus extra to serve

4 tbsp desiccated coconut

1 egg

50 g/1¾ oz polenta

Oil, for deep-frying

In a large bowl, mix together the spring onions, coriander, sweetcorn, chilli powder, chilli sauce, desiccated coconut, egg and polenta until well blended. Cover the bowl with clingfilm and leave to stand for about 10 minutes.

Heat enough oil for deep-frying in a large preheated wok or frying pan to 180–190°C/350–375°F or until a cube of bread browns in 30 seconds.

Carefully drop spoonfuls of the sweetcorn mixture into the hot oil. Deep-fry, in batches, for 4–5 minutes or until crispy and a deep golden brown colour.

Remove the chilli corn balls with a slotted spoon, transfer to kitchen paper and leave to drain thoroughly.

Transfer the chilli corn balls to serving plates and serve with extra sweet chilli sauce for dipping.

Carrot & Coriander Soup

serves 6

15 g/½ oz butter

1½ tbsp sunflower oil

1 onion, finely chopped

4 large carrots, diced

1-cm/½-inch piece
fresh ginger, grated

2 tsp ground coriander

1 tsp plain flour

1.2 litres/2 pints
vegetable stock

150 ml/5 fl oz crème
fraîche

2 tbsp chopped fresh
coriander

Salt and pepper

Croûtons, to serve

Melt the butter with the oil in a saucepan. Add the onion, carrots and ginger, cover and cook over a low heat, stirring occasionally, for 8 minutes until softened and just beginning to colour.

Sprinkle over the ground coriander and flour and cook, stirring constantly, for 1 minute. Gradually stir in the stock, a little at a time, and bring to the boil, stirring constantly. Season to taste with salt and pepper.

Transfer the mixture to the slow cooker, cover and cook on low for 4–5 hours. Ladle the soup into a food processor or blender, in batches if necessary, and process until smooth. Return the soup to the slow cooker and stir in the crème fraîche. Cover and cook on low for a further 15–20 minutes until heated through.

Ladle the soup into warmed soup bowls, sprinkle with the chopped coriander and top with croûtons. Serve immediately.

Tuna Melts

4 slices farmhouse-style bread

280 g/10 oz canned tuna in oil, drained and flaked

4 tbsp mayonnaise, or to taste

1 tbsp Dijon mustard or wholegrain mustard, plus extra to taste

4 spring onions, chopped

2 tbsp finely chopped dill pickle or sweet gerkin, to taste

1 hard-boiled egg, shelled and finely chopped

1 small carrot, grated

1 tbsp rinsed and roughly chopped capers in brine

2 tbsp chopped fresh parsley or snipped fresh chives

4 large lettuce leaves, such as cos

8 thin slices Cheddar cheese

Salt and pepper

Preheat the grill to high. Line a baking tray with foil and set aside.

Toast the bread under the preheated grill for 2 minutes on each side or until crisp and lightly browned.

Meanwhile, put the tuna in a bowl with the mayonnaise and mustard and beat together to break up the tuna. Add the spring onions, pickle, egg, carrot, capers and salt and pepper to taste and beat together, adding extra mayonnaise to taste. Stir in the parsley.

Put the toast on the foil-lined baking tray and top each slice with a lettuce leaf. Divide the tuna salad among the slices of toast and spread out. Top each with 2 cheese slices, cut to fit.

Place under the grill and cook for 2 minutes or until the cheese is melted and lightly browned.

Cut each tuna melt into 4 pieces, transfer to a plate and serve immediately.

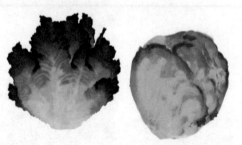

Tex-Mex Bean Dip

serves 4

2 tbsp vegetable oil

1 onion, finely chopped

2 garlic cloves, finely chopped

2–3 fresh green chillies, deseeded and finely chopped

400 g/14 oz canned refried beans or red kidney beans

2 tbsp chilli sauce

6 tbsp hot vegetable stock

115 g/4 oz Cheddar cheese, grated

Salt and pepper

1 fresh red chilli, deseeded and finely chopped, to garnish

Tortilla chips, to serve

Heat the oil in a large, heavy-based frying pan. Add the onion, garlic and green chillies and cook, stirring occasionally, over a low heat for 5 minutes until the onion is soft and translucent. Transfer the mixture to the slow cooker.

Add the refried beans to the slow cooker. If using red kidney beans, drain well and rinse under cold running water. Reserve 2 tablespoons of the beans and mash the remainder roughly with a potato masher. Add all the beans to the slow cooker.

Add the chilli sauce, hot stock and grated cheese, season to taste with salt and pepper and stir well. Cover and cook on low for 2 hours.

Transfer the dip to a serving bowl, garnish with the finely chopped red chilli and serve warm with tortilla chips.

Oyster Rockefeller

serves 4

24 large live oysters

40 g/1½ oz butter

6 spring onions, chopped

1 large garlic clove, crushed

3 tbsp finely chopped celery

40 g/1½ oz watercress sprigs

50 g/1¾ oz young spinach leaves, rinsed and any tough stalks removed

1 tbsp aniseed-flavoured liqueur, such as Pastis

15 g/½ oz fresh breadcrumbs

Few drops of hot pepper sauce, to taste

Salt and pepper

Rock salt and lemon wedges, to serve

Preheat the oven to 200°C/400°F/Gas Mark 6.

Shuck the oysters, running an oyster knife under each oyster to loosen it from its shell. Pour off the liquor. Arrange a 1–2-cm/½–¾-inch layer of rock salt in a roasting tin that is large enough to hold the oysters in a single layer, or use 2 roasting tins. Nestle the oyster shells in the salt so that they remain upright. Cover with a thick, damp tea towel and leave to chill while you make the topping.

If you don't have oyster plates with indentations that hold the shells upright, line 4 plates with a layer of rock salt deep enough to hold 6 shells upright. Set the plates aside.

Melt half the butter in a large frying pan over a medium heat. Add the spring onions, garlic and celery and cook, stirring frequently, for 2–3 minutes until softened.

Stir in the remaining butter, then add the watercress and spinach and cook, stirring constantly, for 1 minute or until the leaves wilt. Transfer to a blender or small food processor and add the liqueur, breadcrumbs, hot pepper sauce and salt and pepper to taste. Whizz until well blended.

Spoon 2–3 teaspoons of the sauce over each oyster. Bake in the preheated oven for 20 minutes. Transfer to the prepared plates and serve with lemon wedges.

Sticky Ginger & Garlic Wings

serves 8-10

1.8 kg/4 lb chicken wings

1 tbsp vegetable oil

1 tsp salt

1 tbsp plain flour

For the sticky ginger & garlic sauce

4 garlic cloves, finely chopped

2 tbsp freshly grated ginger

¼ tsp chilli flakes, or to taste

125 ml/4 fl oz rice vinegar

115 g/4 oz muscovado sugar

1 tsp soy sauce

Preheat the oven to 220°C/425°F/Gas Mark 7.

If the chicken wings being used were frozen and thawed, ensure they're completely dry before starting the recipe. If using whole wings, cut each into 2 pieces. The small wing tips can be saved for a stock or discarded. In a large mixing bowl, toss the wings with the oil and salt. Add the flour and toss until evenly coated.

Line 2 baking trays with lightly greased foil or silicone baking sheets. Divide the wings and spread out evenly without overcrowding. Bake in the preheated oven for 25 minutes, remove from the oven and turn the wings over. Return to the oven and cook for a further 20–30 minutes or until the wings are well browned and cooked through. (Cooking times will vary based on size of the wings. When fully cooked, the bones will easily pull out from the meat.)

Meanwhile, mix all the sauce ingredients in a saucepan. Bring to a simmer, whisking, over a medium heat. Remove from the heat and reserve.

After the wings are cooked, transfer to a large mixing bowl. Pour the warm sauce over the hot wings and toss with a spoon or spatula to completely coat. Leave to rest for 10 minutes, then toss again. The glaze will get sticky and thicken slightly as it cools. Serve warm or at room temperature.

Spinach & Herb Frittata

serves 6-8

4 tbsp olive oil

6 spring onions, sliced

250 g/9 oz young spinach leaves, tough stalks removed, rinsed

6 eggs

3 tbsp finely chopped mixed fresh herbs

2 tbsp freshly grated Parmesan cheese, plus extra to garnish

Salt and pepper

Fresh parsley, to garnish

Heat a 25-cm/10-inch non-stick frying pan with a flameproof handle over a medium heat. Add the oil and heat. Add the spring onions and cook for about 2 minutes.

Add the spinach and cook until it just wilts. Beat the eggs in a large bowl and season with salt and pepper to taste. Using a slotted spoon, transfer the spinach and spring onions to the bowl of eggs and stir in the herbs. Pour the excess oil into a heatproof jug, then scrape off any crusty sediment from the base of the frying pan.

Reheat the frying pan. Add 2 tablespoons of the reserved oil. Pour in the egg mixture, smoothing it into an even layer. Cook, shaking the frying pan occasionally, for 6 minutes or until the base is set when you lift up the side with a fish slice.

Preheat the grill. Sprinkle the top of the frittata with the Parmesan cheese. Place the frying pan under the preheated grill and cook for 3 minutes or until the frittata is set and the cheese is golden.

Remove the frying pan from the heat and slide the frittata onto a serving plate. Leave to stand for at least 5 minutes before cutting and garnishing with extra Parmesan cheese and parsley. Serve hot or at room temperature.

Warm Chickpea Salad

serves 6

200 g/7 oz dried chickpeas, soaked overnight or for at least 5 hours in cold water and drained

100 g/3½ oz stoned black olives

4 spring onions, finely chopped

Fresh parsley sprigs, to garnish

Crusty bread, to serve

For the dressing

2 tbsp red wine vinegar

2 tbsp mixed chopped fresh herbs, such as parsley, rosemary and thyme

3 garlic cloves, very finely chopped

125 ml/4 fl oz extra virgin olive oil

Salt and pepper

Place the chickpeas in a saucepan of fresh water, bring to the boil and boil rapidly for 10 minutes, then drain and rinse. Add the chickpeas to the slow cooker with enough boiling water to cover. Cover and cook on low for 12 hours.

Drain well and transfer to a bowl. Stir in the olives and spring onions.

For the dressing, whisk together the vinegar, herbs and garlic in a measuring jug and season with salt and pepper to taste. Gradually whisk in the olive oil.

Pour the dressing over the still-warm chickpeas and toss lightly to coat. Garnish with the parsley sprigs and serve warm with crusty bread.

Bean & Vegetable Soup

serves 4-6

550 g/1 lb 4 oz dried haricot beans, soaked in cold water overnight or for at least 5 hours, drained and rinsed

2 onions, finely chopped

2 garlic cloves, finely chopped

2 potatoes, chopped

2 carrots, chopped

2 tomatoes, peeled and chopped

2 celery sticks, chopped

4 tbsp extra virgin olive oil

1 bay leaf

2 litres/3½ pints boiling water

Salt and pepper

To garnish

12 black olives

2 tbsp snipped fresh chives

Put the haricot beans into a saucepan of fresh water, bring to the boil and boil rapidly for 10 minutes, then drain and rinse. Put the beans into the slow cooker and add the onions, garlic, potatoes, carrots, tomatoes, celery, olive oil and bay leaf.

Pour in the boiling water, ensuring that all the ingredients are fully submerged. Cover and cook on low for 12 hours until the beans are tender.

Remove and discard the bay leaf. Season the soup to taste with salt and pepper, then stir in the olives and chives.

Ladle into warmed soup bowls and serve.

Warm Crab Dip

400 g/14 oz cream cheese

85 g/3 oz Cheddar cheese, grated

225 g/8 oz crème fraîche or soured cream

4 tbsp mayonnaise

2 tbsp lemon juice

2 tsp Dijon mustard

2 tsp Worcestershire sauce, plus extra to taste

500 g/1 lb 2 oz cooked fresh crabmeat

1 garlic clove, halved

Butter, for greasing

Salt and pepper

Fresh dill sprigs, to garnish

Savoury crackers, to serve

Put the cream cheese into a bowl and stir in the Cheddar cheese, crème fraîche, mayonnaise, lemon juice, mustard and Worcestershire sauce.

Add the crabmeat and salt and pepper to taste and gently stir together. Taste and add extra Worcestershire sauce if wished. Cover and leave to chill for 24 hours.

When you are ready to heat the dip, remove it from the refrigerator and allow it to come to room temperature.

Meanwhile, preheat the oven to 180°C/350°F/Gas Mark 4. Rub the cut sides of the garlic clove over the base and sides of an ovenproof serving dish, then lightly grease.

Spoon the crab mixture into the dish and smooth the surface. Heat the dip through in the preheated oven for 15 minutes. Garnish with the dill sprigs and serve with crackers.

BBQ Chicken Wings

serves 8-10

1.8 kg/4 lb chicken wings

1 tbsp vegetable oil

1 tsp salt

1 tbsp plain flour

Celery sticks and blue cheese dressing, to serve

For the sauce

175 g/6 oz passata

115 g/4 oz unsalted butter, cold, cut into 2.5-cm/1-inch pieces

1½ tbsp white vinegar

¼ tsp Worcestershire sauce

1 tsp hot pepper sauce, or to taste

¼ tsp cayenne pepper

Pinch of garlic powder

Salt

Preheat the oven to 220°C/425°F/Gas Mark 7.

If the chicken wings being used were frozen and thawed, ensure they're completely dry before starting the recipe. If using whole wings, cut each into 2 pieces. The small wing tips can be saved for stock or discarded. In a large mixing bowl, toss the wings with the oil, salt and flour until evenly coated.

Line 2 baking trays with lightly greased foil or silicone baking sheets. Divide the wings and spread out evenly without overcrowding. Bake in the preheated oven for 25 minutes, remove from the oven and turn the wings over. Return to the oven and cook for a further 20–30 minutes or until the wings are well browned and cooked through. (Cooking times will vary based on size of the wings. When fully cooked, the bones will easily pull out from the meat.)

Meanwhile, mix all the sauce ingredients in a saucepan. Bring to a simmer, whisking, over a medium heat. Remove from the heat and reserve. Taste the sauce and adjust the seasoning, adding extra hot pepper sauce and salt if needed.

After the wings are cooked, transfer to a large mixing bowl. Pour the warm sauce over the hot wings and toss with a spoon or spatula to completely coat. Leave to rest for 5 minutes, toss again and serve immediately with celery sticks and a blue cheese dressing on the side.

Bacon & Lentil Soup

serves 4

450 g/1 lb thick, rindless smoked bacon rashers, diced

1 onion, chopped

2 carrots, sliced

2 celery sticks, chopped

1 turnip, chopped

1 large potato, chopped

125 g/4½ oz canned green lentils, rinsed

1 tbsp dried mixed herbs

1 litre/1¾ pints chicken stock or water

Salt and pepper

Heat a large, heavy-based saucepan. Add the bacon and cook over a low heat, stirring frequently, for 4–5 minutes until the fat runs. Add the onion, carrots, celery, turnip and potato and cook, stirring frequently, for 5 minutes.

Add the lentils and mixed herbs and pour in the stock. Bring to the boil, then transfer the mixture to the slow cooker. Cover and cook on low for 8–9 hours or until the lentils are tender.

Season the soup to taste with salt and pepper. Ladle into warmed soup bowls and serve.

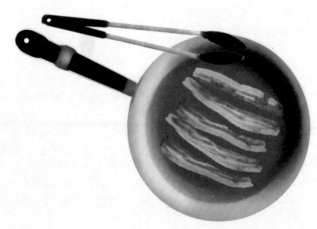

Chicken Satay Skewers with Peanut Sauce

serves 4

4 skinless, boneless chicken breasts, about 115 g/4 oz each, cut into 2-cm/¾-inch cubes

4 tbsp soy sauce

1 tbsp cornflour

2 garlic cloves, finely chopped

2.5-cm/1-inch piece fresh ginger, peeled and finely chopped

85 g/3 oz cucumber, roughly chopped, to serve

For the satay sauce

2 tbsp groundnut or vegetable oil

½ onion, finely chopped

1 garlic clove, finely chopped

4 tbsp crunchy peanut butter

4–5 tbsp water

½ tsp chilli powder

Put the chicken cubes in a shallow dish. Mix the soy sauce, cornflour, garlic and ginger together in a small bowl and pour over the chicken. Cover and leave to marinate in the refrigerator for at least 2 hours.

Meanwhile, soak 12 bamboo skewers in cold water for at least 30 minutes. Preheat the grill. Thread the chicken pieces onto the bamboo skewers. Transfer the skewers to a grill pan and cook under the preheated grill for 3–4 minutes. Turn the skewers over and cook for a further 3–4 minutes or until cooked through.

Meanwhile, make the sauce. Heat the oil in a saucepan, add the onion and garlic, and cook over a medium heat, stirring frequently, for 3–4 minutes until softened. Add the peanut butter, water and chilli powder and simmer for 2–3 minutes until softened and thinned. Serve the skewers immediately with the warm sauce and cucumber.

2

Slow Cooker Favourites

Tagliatelle Bolognese

3 tbsp olive oil

3 bacon rashers, chopped

1 onion, chopped

1 garlic clove, finely chopped

1 carrot, chopped

1 celery stick, chopped

450 g/1 lb beef mince

125 ml/4 fl oz red wine

2 tbsp tomato purée

400 g/14 oz canned chopped tomatoes

300 ml/10 fl oz beef stock

½ tsp dried oregano

1 bay leaf

450 g/1 lb dried tagliatelle

Salt and pepper

Grated Parmesan cheese, to serve

Heat the oil in a saucepan. Add the bacon and cook over a medium heat, stirring frequently, for 3 minutes. Reduce the heat, add the onion, garlic, carrot and celery and cook, stirring occasionally, for 5 minutes until the vegetables have softened.

Increase the heat to medium and add the beef mince. Cook, stirring frequently and breaking it up with a wooden spoon, for 8–10 minutes until evenly browned. Pour in the wine and cook for a few minutes until the alcohol has evaporated, then stir in the tomato purée, tomatoes, stock, oregano and bay leaf and season to taste with salt and pepper.

Bring to the boil, then transfer to the slow cooker. Cover and cook on low for 8–8½ hours.

Shortly before serving, bring a large saucepan of lightly salted water to the boil. Add the pasta, bring back to the boil and cook for 8–10 minutes until tender but still firm to the bite. Drain and put into a warmed serving bowl. Remove and discard the bay leaf, then add the meat sauce to the pasta. Toss with 2 forks, sprinkle with the Parmesan and serve immediately.

Gammon with Black-eyed Beans

serves 4

1 boneless gammon joint, weighing 550 g/1 lb 4 oz

3 tbsp olive oil

1 onion, chopped

2–3 garlic cloves, chopped

2 celery sticks, chopped

1–2 carrots, thinly sliced

1 cinnamon stick

½ tsp ground cloves

¼ tsp freshly grated nutmeg

1 tsp dried oregano

475 ml/16 fl oz chicken or vegetable stock

2 tbsp maple syrup

225 g/8 oz chorizo or other spicy sausages, skinned

400 g/14 oz canned black-eyed beans, drained and rinsed

1 orange pepper, deseeded and chopped

1 tbsp cornflour

2 tbsp water

Pepper

Fresh flat-leaf parsley or oregano sprigs, to garnish

Trim off any fat from the gammon and cut the flesh into 4-cm/1½-inch pieces. Heat 1 tablespoon of the oil in a heavy-based frying pan, add the gammon and cook over a high heat, stirring frequently, for 5 minutes until browned all over. Using a slotted spoon, transfer the gammon to the slow cooker.

Add 1 tablespoon of the remaining oil to the frying pan. Reduce the heat to low, add the onion, garlic, celery and carrots and cook, stirring occasionally, for 5 minutes until the vegetables have softened. Add the cinnamon stick, cloves and nutmeg, season to taste with pepper and cook, stirring constantly, for 2 minutes. Stir in the dried oregano, stock and maple syrup and bring to the boil, stirring constantly. Pour the mixture over the gammon, stir well, cover and cook on low for 5–6 hours.

Heat the remaining oil in a frying pan, add the chorizo and cook, turning frequently, for 10 minutes until browned all over. Remove from the frying pan, cut into chunks and add to the slow cooker with the black-eyed beans and orange pepper. Re-cover and cook on high for 1–1½ hours.

Mix the cornflour and water to a smooth paste in a small bowl, then stir into the stew, re-cover and cook on high for 15 minutes. Remove and discard the cinnamon stick, garnish the stew with parsley sprigs and serve.

Goulash

4 tbsp vegetable oil

650 g/1 lb 7 oz braising steak, cut into 2.5-cm/1-inch cubes

2 tsp plain flour

2 tsp paprika

300 ml/10 fl oz beef stock

3 onions, chopped

4 carrots, diced

1 large potato or 2 medium potatoes, diced

1 bay leaf

1 tsp caraway seeds

400 g/14 oz canned chopped tomatoes

2 tbsp soured cream

Salt and pepper

Heat 2 tablespoons of the oil in a heavy-based frying pan. Add the beef and cook over a medium heat, stirring frequently, until browned all over. Reduce the heat and stir in the flour and paprika. Cook, stirring constantly, for 2 minutes. Gradually stir in the stock and bring to the boil, then transfer the mixture to the slow cooker.

Rinse out the frying pan and heat the remaining oil in it. Add the onions and cook over a low heat, stirring occasionally, for 5 minutes until softened. Stir in the carrots and potato and cook for a few minutes more. Add the bay leaf, caraway seeds and tomatoes. Season to taste with salt and pepper.

Transfer the vegetable mixture to the slow cooker, stir well, then cover and cook on low for 9 hours until the meat is tender.

Remove and discard the bay leaf. Pour the soured cream over the goulash and serve immediately.

Easy Chinese Chicken

serves 4

2 tsp grated fresh ginger

4 garlic cloves, finely chopped

2 star anise

150 ml/5 fl oz Chinese rice wine or medium dry sherry

2 tbsp dark soy sauce

1 tsp sesame oil

5 tbsp water

4 skinless chicken thighs or drumsticks

Shredded spring onions, to garnish

Cooked rice, to serve

Combine the ginger, garlic, star anise, rice wine, soy sauce, sesame oil and water in a bowl. Place the chicken in a saucepan, add the spice mixture and bring to the boil.

Transfer to the slow cooker, cover and cook on low for 4 hours or until the chicken is tender and the juices run clear when a skewer is inserted into the thickest part of the meat.

Remove and discard the star anise. Transfer the chicken to warmed plates, garnish with shredded spring onions and serve immediately with rice.

Summer Vegetable Casserole

serves 4

400 g/14 oz canned cannellini beans, drained and rinsed

400 g/14 oz canned artichoke hearts, drained

1 red pepper, deseeded and sliced

4 small turnips, sliced

225 g/8 oz baby spinach leaves, tough stalks removed

6 fresh thyme sprigs

400 g/14 oz fresh or frozen baby broad beans

1 tbsp olive oil

25 g/1 oz butter

4 shallots, chopped

4 leeks, sliced

3 celery sticks, sliced

3 tbsp plain flour

200 ml/7 fl oz dry white wine

150 ml/5 fl oz vegetable stock

Salt and pepper

Put the cannellini beans, artichoke hearts, red pepper, turnips, spinach and 4 of the thyme sprigs into the slow cooker.

Cook the broad beans in a small saucepan of lightly salted boiling water for 10 minutes, then rinse and drain.

Meanwhile, heat the oil and butter in a large frying pan. Add the shallots, leeks and celery and cook over a low heat, stirring occasionally, for 5 minutes until softened. Stir in the flour and cook, stirring constantly, for 1 minute. Gradually stir in the wine and stock and bring to the boil, stirring constantly. Season to taste with salt and pepper.

Transfer the contents of the frying pan to the slow cooker. Add the broad beans to the slow cooker. Stir well, cover and cook on low for 2½–3 hours. Remove and discard the thyme sprigs. Sprinkle with the leaves from the remaining thyme sprigs and serve immediately.

Venison Casserole

serves 6

3 tbsp olive oil

1 kg/2 lb 4 oz stewing venison, cut into 3-cm/1¼-inch cubes

2 onions, thinly sliced

2 garlic cloves, chopped

350 ml/12 fl oz beef stock

2 tbsp plain flour

125 ml/4 fl oz port

2 tbsp redcurrant jelly

6 juniper berries, crushed

4 cloves, crushed

Pinch of ground cinnamon

Pinch of freshly grated nutmeg

Salt and pepper

Mashed potatoes, to serve

Heat the oil in a heavy-based frying pan. Add the venison and cook over a high heat, stirring frequently, for 5 minutes until browned all over. Using a slotted spoon, transfer to the slow cooker.

Add the onions and garlic to the frying pan, reduce the heat and cook, stirring occasionally, for 5 minutes until softened. Transfer to the slow cooker.

Gradually stir the stock into the frying pan, scraping up any sediment from the base, then bring to the boil, stirring constantly. Sprinkle the flour over the meat in the slow cooker and stir well to coat evenly. Stir in the hot stock, then add the port, redcurrant jelly, juniper berries, cloves, cinnamon and nutmeg. Season to taste with salt and pepper. Cover and cook on low for 7–8 hours until the meat is tender.

Taste and adjust the seasoning if necessary. Remove and discard the cloves, then serve with mashed potatoes.

Chicken Cacciatore

serves 4

3 tbsp olive oil

4 skinless chicken portions, such as breasts, thighs or drumsticks, about 175 g/6 oz each

2 onions, sliced

2 garlic cloves, finely chopped

400 g/14 oz canned chopped tomatoes

1 tbsp tomato purée

2 tbsp chopped fresh parsley

2 tsp fresh thyme leaves, plus extra sprigs to garnish

150 ml/5 fl oz red wine

Salt and pepper

Heat the oil in a heavy-based frying pan. Add the chicken portions and cook over a medium heat, turning occasionally, for 10 minutes until golden all over. Using a slotted spoon, transfer the chicken to the slow cooker.

Add the onions to the frying pan and cook, stirring occasionally, for 5 minutes until softened and just turning golden. Add the garlic, tomatoes, tomato purée, parsley, thyme leaves and wine. Season to taste with salt and pepper and bring to the boil.

Pour the tomato mixture over the chicken portions. Cover and cook on low for 5 hours until the chicken is tender and the juices run clear when a skewer is inserted into the thickest part of the meat. Taste and adjust the seasoning if necessary. Garnish with thyme sprigs and serve.

Pork & Beans

2 tbsp vegetable oil

4 pork chops, trimmed of excess fat

1 onion, chopped

400 g/14 oz canned chopped tomatoes

425 g/15 oz canned baked beans

Butter, for greasing, plus extra for browning (optional)

700 g/1 lb 9 oz potatoes, thinly sliced

425 ml/15 fl oz hot chicken stock

Salt and pepper

Heat the oil in a frying pan. Season the chops well with salt and pepper, add to the frying pan and cook over a medium heat for 2–3 minutes on each side until evenly browned. Remove the frying pan from the heat and transfer the chops to a plate.

Combine the onion, tomatoes and baked beans in a bowl and season well with salt and pepper.

Lightly grease the slow cooker pot, then make a layer of half the potato slices in the base. Cover with half the tomato and bean mixture. Put the chops on top, then add the remaining tomato and bean mixture. Cover with the remaining potato slices. Pour in the stock, cover and cook on low for 8–10 hours or until cooked through.

If wished, dot the topping with butter, then place the slow cooker pot under a preheated grill to brown the potatoes before serving.

Caribbean Beef Stew

serves 6

450 g/1 lb braising steak

450 g/1 lb diced pumpkin, butternut squash or other squash

1 onion, chopped

1 red pepper, deseeded and chopped

2 garlic cloves, finely chopped

2.5-cm/1-inch piece fresh ginger, finely chopped

1 tbsp sweet or hot paprika

225 ml/8 fl oz beef stock

400 g/14 oz canned chopped tomatoes

400 g/14 oz canned chickpeas, drained and rinsed

400 g/14 oz canned black-eyed beans, drained and rinsed

Salt and pepper

Trim off any visible fat from the beef, then dice the meat. Heat a large, heavy-based saucepan without adding any fat. Add the meat and cook, stirring constantly, for a few minutes until evenly browned.

Stir in the pumpkin, onion and red pepper and cook for 1 minute, then add the garlic, ginger and paprika. Pour in the stock, add the tomatoes and bring to the boil.

Transfer the mixture to the slow cooker, cover and cook on low for 7 hours.

Add the chickpeas and black-eyed beans to the stew and season to taste with salt and pepper.

Re-cover and cook on high for 30 minutes. Serve immediately.

Sea Bass in Lemon Sauce

serves 4

8 sea bass fillets

55 g/2 oz unsalted butter

4 tbsp plain flour

850 ml/1½ pints warm milk

4 tbsp lemon juice

225 g/8 oz mushrooms, sliced

1 tbsp dried mixed herbs

2 bay leaves

Salt and pepper

Lemon wedges and cooked asparagus, to serve

Put the fish fillets into the slow cooker and set aside.

Melt the butter in a saucepan over a low heat. Add the flour and cook, stirring constantly, for 1 minute. Gradually stir in the milk, a little at a time, and bring to the boil, stirring constantly.

Stir in the lemon juice and mushrooms, then add the dried mixed herbs and the bay leaves. Season to taste with salt and pepper. Reduce the heat and simmer for 5 minutes. Pour the sauce over the fish fillets, cover and cook on low for 1½ hours.

Carefully lift out the fish fillets and put them on warmed individual plates. Remove and discard the bay leaves and spoon the sauce over the fish. Serve immediately with lemon wedges and asparagus.

Risotto with Spring Vegetables

serves 4

1.2 litres/2 pints vegetable stock

Large pinch of saffron threads

55 g/2 oz butter

1 tbsp olive oil

1 onion, chopped

2 garlic cloves, finely chopped

225 g/8 oz risotto rice

3 tbsp dry white wine

1 bay leaf

250 g/9 oz mixed spring vegetables, such as asparagus spears, green beans, baby carrots, baby broad beans and petits pois, thawed if frozen

2 tbsp chopped fresh flat-leaf parsley

55 g/2 oz Parmesan cheese, grated

Salt and pepper

Put 100 ml/3½ fl oz of the stock into a small bowl, crumble in the saffron threads and leave to infuse. Reserve 150 ml/5 fl oz of the remaining stock and heat the remainder in a saucepan.

Meanwhile, melt half the butter with the oil in a separate large saucepan. Add the onion and garlic and cook over a low heat, stirring occasionally, for 5 minutes until softened. Stir in the rice and cook, stirring constantly, for 1–2 minutes until all the grains are coated and glistening. Pour in the wine and cook, stirring constantly, for a few minutes until all the alcohol has evaporated. Season to taste with salt and pepper. Pour in the hot stock and the saffron mixture, add the bay leaf and bring to the boil, stirring constantly.

Transfer the mixture to the slow cooker, cover and cook on low for 2 hours. Meanwhile, if using fresh vegetables, slice the asparagus spears, green beans and carrots and blanch all the vegetables in boiling water for 5 minutes. Drain and reserve.

Stir the reserved stock into the rice mixture if it seems dry and add the mixed vegetables, sprinkling them evenly over the top. Re-cover and cook on low for a further 30–45 minutes until heated through.

Remove and discard the bay leaf. Gently stir in the parsley, the remaining butter and the Parmesan and serve immediately.

Sweet & Sour Pasta

serves 4

4 tbsp olive oil

1 large red onion, sliced

2 garlic cloves, finely chopped

2 red peppers, deseeded and sliced

2 courgettes, cut into batons

1 aubergine, cut into batons

450 ml/16 fl oz passata

150 ml/5 fl oz water

4 tbsp lemon juice

2 tbsp balsamic vinegar

55 g/2 oz stoned black olives, sliced

1 tbsp sugar

400 g/14 oz dried pappardelle pasta

Salt and pepper

Fresh flat-leaf parsley leaves, to garnish

Heat the oil in a large, heavy-based saucepan. Add the onion, garlic and red peppers and cook over a low heat, stirring occasionally, for 5 minutes. Add the courgettes and aubergine and cook, stirring occasionally, for a further 5 minutes. Stir in the passata and water and bring to the boil. Stir in the lemon juice, vinegar, olives and sugar and season to taste with salt and pepper.

Transfer the mixture to the slow cooker. Cover and cook on low for 5 hours until all the vegetables are tender.

Shortly before serving, bring a large saucepan of lightly salted water to the boil. Add the pasta, bring back to the boil and cook for 8–10 minutes until tender but still firm to the bite. Drain and transfer to a warmed serving dish, then spoon the vegetable mixture over the pasta and toss lightly. Garnish with parsley leaves and serve immediately.

Traditional Pot Roast

serves 6

1 onion, finely chopped

4 carrots, sliced

4 baby turnips, sliced

4 celery sticks, sliced

2 potatoes, sliced

1 sweet potato, sliced

1.3–1.8 kg/3–4 lb boned and rolled beef brisket

2 bay leaves

1 tbsp dried mixed herbs

300 ml/10 fl oz boiling beef stock

Salt and pepper

Place the onion, carrots, turnips, celery, potatoes and sweet potato in the slow cooker and stir to mix well.

Rub the beef all over with salt and pepper, then place on top of the bed of vegetables. Add the bay leaves and mixed herbs and pour in the stock. Cover and cook on low for 9–10 hours until the beef is cooked to your liking.

Remove the beef, carve into slices and arrange on serving plates. Remove and discard the bay leaves. Spoon the vegetables and cooking juices onto the plates and serve.

Vegetable Curry

serves 4-6

2 tbsp vegetable oil

1 tsp cumin seeds

1 onion, sliced

2 curry leaves

2.5-cm/1-inch piece fresh ginger, finely chopped

2 fresh red chillies, deseeded and chopped

2 tbsp curry paste

2 carrots, sliced

115 g/4 oz mangetout

1 head cauliflower, cut into florets

3 tomatoes, peeled and chopped

85 g/3 oz frozen peas, thawed

½ tsp ground turmeric

150–225 ml/5–8 fl oz boiling vegetable or chicken stock

Salt and pepper

Heat the oil in a large, heavy-based saucepan. Add the cumin seeds and cook, stirring constantly, for 1–2 minutes until they give off their aroma and begin to pop. Add the onion and curry leaves and cook, stirring occasionally, for 5 minutes until the onion has softened. Add the ginger and chillies and cook, stirring occasionally, for 1 minute.

Stir in the curry paste and cook, stirring, for 2 minutes, then add the carrots, mangetout and cauliflower florets. Cook for 5 minutes, then add the tomatoes, peas and turmeric and season to taste with salt and pepper. Cook for 3 minutes, then add 150 ml/5 fl oz of the stock and bring to the boil.

Transfer the mixture to the slow cooker. If the vegetables are not covered, add more hot stock, then cover and cook on low for 5 hours until tender. Remove and discard the curry leaves before serving.

Chipotle Chicken

4–6 dried chipotle chillies

4 garlic cloves, unpeeled

1 small onion, chopped

400 g/14 oz canned chopped tomatoes

300 ml/10 fl oz chicken or vegetable stock

4 chicken breasts, about 175 g/6 oz each

Salt and pepper

Chopped fresh coriander, to garnish

Preheat the oven to 200°C/400°F/Gas Mark 6.

Place the chillies in a bowl and pour in just enough hot water to cover. Set aside to soak for 30 minutes.

Meanwhile, place the unpeeled garlic cloves on a baking tray and roast in the preheated oven for about 10 minutes until soft. Remove from the oven and leave to cool.

Drain the chillies, reserving 125 ml/4 fl oz of the soaking water. Seed the chillies, if wished, and roughly chop. Place the chillies and reserved soaking water in a blender or food processor and process to a purée. Peel and mash the garlic in a bowl.

Place the chilli purée, garlic, onion and tomatoes in the slow cooker and stir in the stock. Season the chicken with salt and pepper and place in the slow cooker. Cover and cook on low for about 5 hours until the chicken is tender and the juices run clear when a skewer is inserted into the thickest part of the meat.

Lift the chicken out of the slow cooker with a slotted spoon, cover and keep warm. Pour the cooking liquid into a saucepan and bring to the boil on the hob. Boil for 5–10 minutes until reduced. Place the chicken on warmed plates and spoon the sauce over it. Garnish with chopped coriander and serve immediately.

Pork with Peppers & Apricots

serves 4

2 tbsp olive oil

4 pork chops, trimmed of excess fat

1 shallot, chopped

2 garlic cloves, finely chopped

2 orange peppers, deseeded and sliced

1 tbsp plain flour

600 ml/1 pint chicken stock

1 tbsp medium–hot Indian curry paste

115 g/4 oz ready-to-eat dried apricots

Salt and pepper

Baby spinach leaves and cooked couscous, to serve

Heat the oil in a large frying pan. Add the chops and cook over a medium heat for 2–4 minutes on each side until evenly browned. Remove with tongs and put them into the slow cooker.

Add the shallot, garlic and orange peppers to the frying pan, reduce the heat and cook, stirring occasionally, for 5 minutes until softened. Stir in the flour and cook, stirring constantly, for 1 minute. Gradually stir in the stock, a little at a time, then add the curry paste and apricots. Bring to the boil, stirring occasionally.

Season to taste with salt and pepper and transfer the mixture to the slow cooker. Cover and cook on low for 8–9 hours until the meat is tender. Serve immediately with baby spinach and couscous.

Stuffed Cabbage with Tomato Sauce

serves 6

225 g/8 oz finely ground mixed nuts

2 onions, finely chopped

1 garlic clove, finely chopped

2 celery sticks, finely chopped

115 g/4 oz Cheddar cheese, grated

1 tsp finely chopped fresh thyme

2 eggs

1 tsp yeast extract

12 large green cabbage leaves

For the tomato sauce

2 tbsp sunflower oil

2 onions, chopped

2 garlic cloves, finely chopped

600 g/1 lb 5 oz canned chopped tomatoes

2 tbsp tomato purée

1½ tsp sugar

1 bay leaf

Salt and pepper

First, make the tomato sauce. Heat the oil in a heavy-based saucepan. Add the onions and cook over a medium heat, stirring occasionally, for 5 minutes until softened. Stir in the garlic and cook for 1 minute, then add the tomatoes, tomato purée, sugar and bay leaf. Season to taste with salt and pepper and bring to the boil. Reduce the heat and simmer gently for 20 minutes until thickened.

Meanwhile, combine the nuts, onions, garlic, celery, cheese and thyme in a bowl. Lightly beat the eggs with the yeast extract in a jug, then stir into the nut mixture. Set aside.

Cut out the thick stalk from the cabbage leaves. Blanch the leaves in a large saucepan of boiling water for 5 minutes, then drain and refresh under cold water. Pat dry with kitchen paper.

Place a little of the nut mixture on the stalk end of each cabbage leaf. Fold the sides over, then roll up to make a neat parcel.

Arrange the cabbage rolls in the slow cooker, seam-side down. Remove and discard the bay leaf from the tomato sauce and pour the sauce over the cabbage rolls. Cover and cook on low for 3–4 hours. Serve the cabbage rolls hot or cold.

Sea Bass with Fennel & Orange Juice

serves 4

4 whole sea bass, about 350 g/12 oz each, gutted and cleaned

1 orange, halved and thinly sliced

2 garlic cloves, thinly sliced

6 fresh thyme sprigs

1 tbsp olive oil

1 fennel bulb, thinly sliced

450 ml/16 fl oz orange juice

1 bay leaf

1 tsp dill seeds

Salt and pepper

Salad leaves, to serve

Season the fish inside and outside with salt and pepper. Make 3–4 diagonal slashes on each side. Divide the orange slices between the cavities and add 2–3 garlic slices and a thyme sprig to each. Chop the remaining thyme sprigs and put in the slashes with the remaining garlic slices.

Heat the oil in a large frying pan. Add the fennel and cook over a medium heat, stirring frequently, for 3–5 minutes until just softened. Add the orange juice and bay leaf and bring to the boil, then reduce the heat and simmer for 5 minutes.

Transfer the fennel mixture to the slow cooker. Put the fish on top and sprinkle with the dill seeds. Cover and cook on high for 1¼–1½ hours until the flesh flakes easily.

Carefully transfer the fish to 4 warmed plates. Remove and discard the bay leaf and spoon the fennel and some of the cooking juices over the fish. Serve immediately with salad leaves.

Vegetable Stew with Dumplings

½ butternut squash, peeled, deseeded and cut into chunks

2 onions, sliced

2 potatoes, cut into chunks

2 carrots, roughly chopped

2 celery sticks, sliced

2 courgettes, sliced

2 tbsp tomato purée

600 ml/1 pint hot vegetable stock

1 bay leaf

1 tsp ground coriander

½ tsp dried thyme

400 g/14 oz canned sweetcorn kernels, drained

Salt and pepper

Fresh flat-leaf parsley sprigs, to garnish

For the dumplings
200 g/7 oz self-raising flour

Pinch of salt

115 g/4 oz vegetable suet

2 tbsp chopped fresh parsley

About 125 ml/4 fl oz milk

Put the butternut squash, onions, potatoes, carrots, celery and courgettes into the slow cooker. Stir the tomato purée into the stock and pour it over the vegetables. Add the bay leaf, ground coriander and thyme and season to taste with salt and pepper. Cover and cook on low for 6 hours.

To make the dumplings, sift the flour and salt into a bowl and stir in the vegetable suet and parsley. Add just enough milk to make a firm but light dough. Knead lightly and shape into 12 small balls.

Stir the sweetcorn into the vegetable stew and place the dumplings on top. Cook on high for 30 minutes.

Transfer to serving plates and garnish with parsley sprigs. Serve immediately.

Duck & Red Wine Stew

serves 4

4 duck portions, about 175 g/6 oz each

1 red onion, chopped

2–3 garlic cloves, chopped

1 large carrot, chopped

2 celery sticks, chopped

2 tbsp plain flour

300 ml/10 fl oz red wine

2 tbsp brandy

175 ml/6 fl oz chicken stock or water

7.5-cm/3-inch strip thinly pared orange rind

2 tbsp redcurrant jelly

115 g/4 oz sugar snap peas

1–2 tsp olive oil

115 g/4 oz button mushrooms

Salt and pepper

Chopped fresh flat-leaf parsley, to garnish

Heat a heavy-based frying pan for 1 minute, then add the duck portions and cook over a low heat until the fat runs. Increase the heat to medium and cook, turning once, for 5 minutes until browned on both sides. Using a slotted spoon, transfer to the slow cooker.

Add the onion, garlic, carrot and celery to the frying pan and cook, stirring occasionally, for 5 minutes until softened. Sprinkle in the flour and cook, stirring constantly, for 2 minutes, then remove the frying pan from the heat. Gradually stir in the wine, brandy and stock, return the frying pan to the heat and bring to the boil, stirring constantly. Season to taste with salt and pepper and stir in the orange rind and redcurrant jelly.

Pour the mixture over the duck portions in the slow cooker, cover and cook on low, occasionally skimming off the fat from the stew, for 8 hours.

Cook the sugar snap peas in a saucepan of boiling water for 3 minutes, then drain. Heat the oil in a separate saucepan, add the mushrooms and cook, stirring frequently, for 3 minutes. Add the sugar snap peas and mushrooms to the stew, re-cover and cook on high for 25–30 minutes until tender. Garnish with parsley and serve immediately.

Three Bean Chilli

serves 4-6

115 g/4 oz dried red kidney beans, soaked overnight or for at least 5 hours, drained and rinsed

115 g/4 oz dried black beans, soaked overnight or for at least 5 hours, drained and rinsed

115 g/4 oz dried pinto beans, soaked overnight or for at least 5 hours, drained and rinsed

2 tbsp vegetable oil

1 onion, chopped

1 garlic clove, finely chopped

1 fresh red chilli, deseeded and chopped

1 yellow pepper, deseeded and chopped

1 tsp ground cumin

1 tbsp chilli powder

1 litre/1¾ pints vegetable stock

1 tbsp sugar

Salt and pepper

Chopped fresh coriander, to garnish

Put all the beans in a saucepan with fresh water to cover, bring to the boil and boil for 10 minutes. Drain, rinse well with fresh water and set aside.

Heat the oil in a large, heavy-based saucepan. Add the onion, garlic, chilli and yellow pepper and cook over a medium heat, stirring occasionally, for 5 minutes. Stir in the cumin and chilli powder and cook, stirring, for 1–2 minutes. Add the drained beans and stock and bring to the boil. Boil vigorously for 15 minutes.

Transfer the mixture to the slow cooker, cover and cook on low for 10 hours until the beans are tender.

Season the mixture to taste with salt and pepper, then ladle about a third into a bowl. Mash well with a potato masher, then return the mashed beans to the slow cooker and stir in the sugar. Serve immediately, sprinkled with chopped coriander.

Chicken & Mushroom Stew

serves 4

15 g/½ oz butter

2 tbsp olive oil

4 skinless chicken portions, such as breasts, thighs or drumsticks, about 175 g/6 oz each

2 red onions, sliced

2 garlic cloves, finely chopped

400 g/14 oz canned chopped tomatoes

2 tbsp chopped fresh flat-leaf parsley

6 fresh basil leaves, torn

1 tbsp sun-dried tomato paste

150 ml/5 fl oz red wine

300 g/10½ oz mushrooms, sliced

Salt and pepper

Heat the butter and oil in a heavy-based frying pan. Add the chicken, in batches if necessary, and cook over a medium–high heat, turning frequently, for 10 minutes until golden brown all over. Using a slotted spoon, transfer the chicken to the slow cooker.

Add the onions and garlic to the frying pan and cook over a low heat, stirring occasionally, for 10 minutes until translucent. Stir in the tomatoes, parsley, basil, sun-dried tomato paste and wine. Season to taste with salt and pepper. Bring to the boil, then pour the mixture over the chicken.

Cover the slow cooker and cook on low for 6½ hours. Stir in the mushrooms, re-cover and cook on high for 30 minutes until the chicken and vegetables are tender and the juices run clear when a skewer is inserted into the thickest part of the meat. Taste and adjust the seasoning if necessary, then serve.

Lentil & Vegetable Casserole

serves 4

1 onion

10 cloves

200 g/7 oz canned green lentils, drained and rinsed

1 bay leaf

1.5 litres/2½ pints boiling vegetable stock

2 leeks, sliced

2 potatoes, diced

2 carrots, chopped

3 courgettes, sliced

1 celery stick, sliced

1 red pepper, deseeded and chopped

1 tbsp lemon juice

Salt and pepper

Peel the onion, stud it with the cloves and place it in the slow cooker. Add the lentils and bay leaf. Pour in the stock, cover and cook on high for 1½–2 hours.

Remove the onion with a slotted spoon and re-cover the slow cooker. Remove and discard the cloves and slice the onion. Add the onion, leeks, potatoes, carrots, courgettes, celery and red pepper to the lentils and season to taste with salt and pepper. Re-cover and cook on high for 3–4 hours until all the vegetables are tender.

Remove and discard the bay leaf and stir in the lemon juice. Taste and adjust the seasoning if necessary, then serve.

Pork with Apple & Herbs

serves 6

2 tbsp plain flour

800 g/1 lb 12 oz boneless pork, cut into 2.5-cm/1-inch cubes

5 tbsp sunflower oil

1 large onion, chopped

2 garlic cloves, finely chopped

2 eating apples, cored and cut into wedges

300 ml/10 fl oz cider or apple juice

600 ml/1 pint chicken stock

2 bay leaves

2 fresh sage sprigs

1 fresh rosemary sprig

3 tbsp chopped fresh parsley

Salt and pepper

Mashed potatoes, to serve

Put the flour into a plastic food bag and season well with salt and pepper. Add the pork cubes, in batches, hold the top securely and shake well to coat. Transfer the meat to a plate.

Heat 3 tablespoons of the oil in a large frying pan. Add the pork cubes, in batches if necessary, and cook over a medium heat, stirring frequently, for 5–8 minutes until evenly browned. Transfer to a plate and set aside.

Add the remaining oil to the frying pan and heat. Add the onion and garlic and cook over a low heat, stirring occasionally, for 10 minutes until softened and lightly browned. Add the apple wedges and cook, stirring occasionally, for 3–5 minutes until beginning to colour. Gradually stir in the cider and stock, scraping up any sediment from the base of the frying pan, and bring to the boil. Season to taste with salt and pepper, add the bay leaves and the sage and rosemary sprigs and transfer to the slow cooker. Stir in the pork, cover and cook on low for 6–7 hours.

Remove and discard the bay leaves, sage and rosemary. Transfer the stew to warmed individual plates and sprinkle with the parsley. Serve immediately with mashed potatoes.

Neapolitan Beef

serves 6

300 ml/10 fl oz red wine

4 tbsp olive oil

1 celery stick, chopped

2 shallots, sliced

4 garlic cloves, finely chopped

1 bay leaf

10 fresh basil leaves, plus extra to garnish

3 fresh parsley sprigs

Pinch of grated nutmeg

Pinch of ground cinnamon

2 cloves

1.5 kg/3 lb 5 oz boned and rolled beef brisket

1–2 garlic cloves, thinly sliced

2 streaky bacon rashers, chopped

400 g/14 oz canned chopped tomatoes

2 tbsp tomato purée

Combine the wine, half the oil, the celery, shallots, garlic, herbs and spices in a large, non-metallic bowl. Add the beef, cover and leave to marinate in the refrigerator, turning occasionally, for 12 hours.

Drain the beef, reserving the marinade, and pat dry with kitchen paper. Make small incisions all over the beef using a sharp knife. Insert a slice of garlic and a piece of bacon in each pocket. Heat the remaining oil in a large frying pan. Add the meat and cook over a medium heat, turning frequently, until browned. Transfer to the slow cooker.

Strain the reserved marinade into the frying pan and bring to the boil. Stir in the tomatoes and tomato purée. Stir well, then pour the mixture over the beef. Cover and cook on low for about 8–9 hours until the beef is cooked to your liking. If possible, turn the beef over halfway through the cooking time and re-cover the slow cooker immediately.

Remove the beef from the slow cooker and place on a carving board. Cover with foil and leave to stand for 10–15 minutes. Cut into slices and transfer to a serving platter. Spoon over the sauce, garnish with basil leaves and serve immediately.

Spicy Chicken with Sausage & Peppers

1½ tbsp plain flour

4 skinless chicken portions, such as breasts, thighs or drumsticks, about 175 g/6 oz each

2 tbsp olive oil, plus extra if needed

1 onion, chopped

2–3 garlic cloves, chopped

1 fresh red chilli, deseeded and chopped

225 g/8 oz chorizo or other spicy sausages, skinned and cut into small chunks

300 ml/10 fl oz chicken stock

150 ml/5 fl oz dry white wine

1 tbsp dark soy sauce

1 large red pepper, deseeded and sliced into rings

250 g/9 oz fresh or frozen broad beans

Large handful of rocket or baby spinach leaves

Salt and pepper

Spread out the flour on a plate and season well with salt and pepper. Toss the chicken in the seasoned flour until thoroughly coated, shaking off any excess. Reserve any remaining flour.

Heat 1 tablespoon of the oil in a heavy-based frying pan, add the chicken portions and cook over a medium–high heat, turning frequently, for 10 minutes or until golden brown all over. Add a little more oil during cooking if necessary. Using a slotted spoon, transfer the chicken portions to the slow cooker.

Add the remaining tablespoon of oil to the frying pan. Add the onion, garlic and chilli and cook over a low heat, stirring occasionally, for 5 minutes until softened. Add the chorizo and cook, stirring frequently, for a further 2 minutes. Sprinkle in the reserved flour and cook, stirring constantly, for 2 minutes, then remove the frying pan from the heat. Gradually stir in the stock, wine and soy sauce, then return the frying pan to the heat and bring to the boil, stirring constantly. Pour the onion mixture over the chicken, then cover and cook on low for 6½ hours.

Add the red pepper and broad beans to the slow cooker, re-cover and cook on high for 45–60 minutes until the chicken and vegetables are tender and the juices run clear when a skewer is inserted into the thickest part of the meat. Season to taste with salt and pepper, stir in the rocket and leave to stand for 2 minutes until just wilted, then serve.

Jalapeño Pork Chops

4 pork chops, trimmed of excess fat

2 tbsp vegetable oil

450 g/1 lb canned pineapple chunks in juice

1 red pepper, deseeded and finely chopped

2 fresh jalapeño chillies, deseeded and finely chopped

1 onion, finely chopped

1 tbsp chopped fresh coriander, plus extra sprigs to garnish

125 ml/4 fl oz hot chicken stock

Salt and pepper

Flour tortillas, to serve

Season the chops with salt and pepper to taste. Heat the oil in a large, heavy-based frying pan. Add the chops and cook over a medium heat for 2–3 minutes each side until lightly browned. Transfer to the slow cooker. Drain the pineapple, reserving the juice, and set aside.

Add the red pepper, chillies and onion to the frying pan and cook, stirring occasionally, for 5 minutes until the onion has softened. Transfer the mixture to the slow cooker and add the chopped coriander, stock and 125 ml/4 fl oz of the reserved pineapple juice. Cover and cook on low for 6 hours until the chops are tender.

Add the reserved pineapple to the slow cooker, re-cover and cook on high for 15 minutes. Garnish with coriander sprigs and serve immediately with flour tortillas.

Chicken with New Potatoes & Bacon

serves 6

1 chicken, weighing
1.8 kg/4 lb

55 g/2 oz butter

2 tbsp olive oil

650 g/1 lb 7 oz baby
onions, peeled

650 g/1 lb 7 oz small
new potatoes

6 bacon rashers,
chopped

500 ml/18 fl oz dry
white wine

1 bay leaf

1 tbsp dried mixed
herbs

500 ml/18 fl oz hot
chicken stock

Salt and pepper

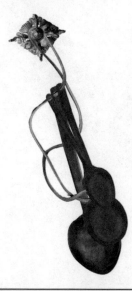

Season the chicken inside and out with salt and pepper.
Melt half the butter with the oil in a large frying pan.
Add the chicken and cook over a medium heat, turning
frequently, for 8–10 minutes, until evenly browned.
Remove from the pan and put it into the slow cooker,
breast-side down.

Add the onions, potatoes and bacon to the frying pan and
cook, stirring frequently, for 10 minutes until lightly
browned. Pour in the wine, season to taste with salt and
pepper and add the bay leaf and mixed herbs. Bring to the
boil, then transfer the mixture to the slow cooker. Pour in
the hot stock. Cover and cook, turning the chicken once
halfway through cooking, for 5–6 hours until the chicken
is tender and the juices run clear when a skewer is inserted
into the thickest part of the meat.

Using a slotted spoon, transfer the vegetables and bacon
to a bowl. Carefully remove the chicken and put it on a
warmed serving dish. Remove and discard the bay leaf.

Measure 600 ml/1 pint of the cooking liquid, pour it into
a pan and bring to the boil. Boil until slightly reduced, then
whisk in the remaining butter a little at a time. Pour the
sauce into a sauceboat. Carve the chicken and transfer to
individual plates with the bacon and vegetables. Serve
immediately with the sauce.

Gammon Cooked in Cider

serves 6

1 boneless gammon joint, weighing 1 kg/2 lb 4 oz

1 onion, halved

4 cloves

6 black peppercorns

1 tsp juniper berries

1 celery stick, chopped

1 carrot, sliced

1 litre/1¾ pints cider

Place a trivet or rack in the slow cooker if you wish and stand the gammon on it. Otherwise, just place the gammon in the slow cooker. Stud each of the onion halves with 2 cloves and add to the slow cooker with the peppercorns, juniper berries, celery and carrot.

Pour in the cider, cover and cook on low for 8 hours until the meat is tender.

Remove the gammon from the slow cooker and place on a board. Cover with foil and leave to stand for 10–15 minutes. Discard the cooking liquid and flavourings.

Cut off any rind and fat from the gammon, then carve into slices and serve immediately.

Slow Cooker Salmon

150 ml/5 fl oz fish stock

225 ml/8 fl oz dry white wine

2 lemons

1 onion, thinly sliced

4 salmon fillets, about 175 g/6 oz each

1 tbsp dried mixed herbs

1.3 kg/3 lb spinach, tough stalks removed

Freshly grated nutmeg, to taste

175 g/6 oz unsalted butter, plus extra for greasing

Salt and pepper

Lightly grease a slow cooker pot with butter. Pour the stock and wine into a saucepan and bring to the boil. Meanwhile, thinly slice 1 of the lemons. Arrange half the lemon slices and all the onion slices over the base of the slow cooker and top with the salmon fillets. Season to taste with salt and pepper, add the mixed herbs and cover the fish with the remaining lemon slices. Pour the hot stock mixture over the fish, cover and cook on low for 1½ hours until the fish flakes easily.

Meanwhile, grate the rind and squeeze the juice from the remaining lemon. When the fish is nearly ready, cook the spinach, in just the water clinging to the leaves after washing, for 3–5 minutes until wilted. Drain well, squeezing out as much water as possible. Chop finely, arrange on warmed individual plates and season to taste with salt, pepper and nutmeg.

Carefully lift the fish out of the slow cooker and discard the lemon and onion slices. Put the salmon fillets on top of the spinach and keep warm.

Melt the butter in a saucepan over a low heat. Stir in the lemon rind and half the juice. Taste and adjust the seasoning, adding more lemon juice, salt and pepper if needed. Pour the lemon butter sauce over the fish and serve immediately.

Nutty Chicken

3 tbsp sunflower oil

4 skinless chicken portions

2 shallots, chopped

1 tsp ground ginger

1 tbsp plain flour

425 ml/15 fl oz beef stock

55 g/2 oz walnut pieces

Grated rind of 1 lemon

2 tbsp lemon juice

1 tbsp black treacle

Salt and pepper

Fresh watercress or mizuna sprigs, to garnish

Heat the oil in a large, heavy-based frying pan. Season the chicken portions with salt and pepper and add to the frying pan. Cook over a medium heat, turning occasionally, for 5–8 minutes until lightly golden all over. Transfer to the slow cooker.

Add the shallots to the frying pan and cook, stirring occasionally, for 3–4 minutes until softened. Sprinkle in the ginger and flour and cook, stirring constantly, for 1 minute. Gradually stir in the stock and bring to the boil, stirring constantly. Reduce the heat and simmer for 1 minute, then stir in the walnuts, lemon rind and juice and treacle.

Pour the sauce over the chicken. Cover and cook on low for 6 hours until the chicken is tender and the juices run clear when a skewer is inserted into the thickest part of the meat. Taste and adjust the seasoning if necessary. Transfer the chicken to warmed bowls and spoon over the sauce. Garnish with watercress sprigs and serve immediately.

Rich Beef & Coffee Stew

4 tbsp sunflower oil

1.3 kg/3 lb braising steak, cut into 2.5-cm/1-inch cubes

4 onions, sliced

1 garlic clove, finely chopped

5 tbsp plain flour

300 ml/10 fl oz red wine

Pinch of dried oregano

1 small fresh rosemary sprig

500 ml/18 fl oz black coffee

Salt and pepper

Fresh marjoram sprigs, to garnish

Mashed sweet potatoes, to serve

Heat the oil in a large frying pan. Add the beef and cook over a medium heat, stirring frequently, for 8–10 minutes, until evenly browned. Transfer to the slow cooker with a slotted spoon.

Add the onions and garlic to the frying pan, reduce the heat and cook, stirring occasionally, for 10 minutes until softened and just beginning to colour. Stir in the flour and cook, stirring constantly, for 1 minute. Gradually stir in the wine, a little at a time. Add the oregano and rosemary sprig and season to taste with salt and pepper. Pour in the coffee and bring to the boil, stirring constantly.

Transfer the mixture to the slow cooker. Cover and cook on low for 8–9 hours until the meat is tender. Remove and discard the rosemary sprig. Taste and adjust the seasoning, adding salt and pepper if needed. Garnish with marjoram sprigs and serve with mashed sweet potatoes.

Chicken in Mushroom & White Wine Sauce

serves 4-6

2 tbsp plain flour

1 chicken, weighing
1.6 kg/3 lb 8 oz, cut into
8 pieces

55 g/2 oz unsalted
butter

1 tbsp sunflower oil

4 shallots, finely
chopped

12 button mushrooms,
sliced

2 tbsp brandy

500 ml/18 fl oz dry
white wine

250 ml/9 fl oz double
cream

Salt and pepper

Put the flour into a plastic food bag and season to taste. Add the chicken pieces, in batches, hold the top securely and shake well to coat. Transfer the chicken to a plate.

Heat half the butter with the oil in a heavy-based frying pan. Add the chicken pieces and cook over a medium–high heat, turning frequently, for 10 minutes until golden all over. Using a slotted spoon, transfer them to a plate.

Wipe out the pan with kitchen paper, then return to a medium–high heat and melt the remaining butter. Add the shallots and mushrooms and cook, stirring constantly, for 3 minutes. Return the chicken to the pan and remove it from the heat. Warm the brandy in a small pan, ignite and pour it over the chicken, shaking the frying pan gently until the flames have died down.

Return to the heat and pour in the wine. Bring to the boil, scraping any sediment from the base of the pan. Transfer to the slow cooker, cover and cook on low for 5–6 hours until the chicken is tender and the juices run clear when a skewer is inserted into the thickest part of the meat.

Transfer the chicken to a serving dish. Skim off any fat from the surface of the cooking liquid and pour the liquid into a saucepan. Stir in the cream and bring just to the boil over a low heat and pour over the chicken. Serve immediately.

Courgettes with Peppers & Tomatoes

serves 6

1 kg/2 lb 4 oz courgettes, thickly sliced

1 onion, finely chopped

2 garlic cloves, finely chopped

2 red peppers, deseeded and chopped

5 tbsp hot vegetable stock

4 tomatoes, peeled and chopped

25 g/1 oz butter, diced

Salt and cayenne pepper

Place the courgettes, onion, garlic and red peppers in the slow cooker and season to taste with salt and cayenne pepper.

Pour in the stock and mix well.

Sprinkle the chopped tomatoes on top and dot with the butter. Cover and cook on high for 2½ hours until tender. Serve immediately.

Beef Stew with Olives

serves 4-6

900 g/2 lb braising steak, cubed

2 onions, thinly sliced

2 carrots, sliced

4 large garlic cloves, lightly crushed

1 bouquet garni

4 juniper berries

500 ml/18 fl oz dry red wine

2 tbsp brandy

2 tbsp olive oil

3 tbsp plain flour

175 g/6 oz lardons or diced bacon

2 x 10-cm/4-inch strips thinly pared orange rind

85 g/3 oz stoned black olives, rinsed

Salt and pepper

Chopped fresh flat-leaf parsley and finely grated orange rind, to garnish

Cooked tagliatelle, to serve

Put the braising steak in a large, non-metallic dish. Add the onions, carrots, garlic, bouquet garni and juniper berries. Season to taste with salt and pepper. Combine the wine, brandy and olive oil in a jug and pour the mixture over the meat and vegetables. Cover with clingfilm and leave to marinate in the refrigerator for 24 hours.

Using a slotted spoon, remove the steak from the marinade and pat dry with kitchen paper. Reserve the marinade, vegetables and flavourings. Place the flour in a shallow dish and season well with salt and pepper. Toss the steak cubes in the flour until well coated and shake off any excess.

Sprinkle half the lardons in the base of the slow cooker and top with the steak cubes. Pour in the marinade, including the vegetables and flavourings, then add the strips of orange rind and the olives. Top with the remaining lardons. Cover and cook on low for 9½–10 hours until the steak and vegetables are tender.

Remove and discard the bouquet garni and skim off any fat that has risen to the surface of the stew. Sprinkle the parsley and grated orange rind over the top and serve with cooked tagliatelle.

Lamb Stew with Red Peppers

serves 4

1½ tbsp plain flour

1 tsp ground cloves

450 g/1 lb boneless lamb, cut into thin strips

1–1½ tbsp olive oil

1 onion, sliced

2–3 garlic cloves, sliced

300 ml/10 fl oz orange juice

150 ml/5 fl oz lamb or chicken stock

1 cinnamon stick

2 red peppers, deseeded and sliced into rings

4 tomatoes, roughly chopped

4 fresh coriander sprigs

Salt and pepper

Mashed sweet potatoes and cooked green beans, to serve

Combine the flour and ground cloves in a shallow dish, add the strips of lamb and toss well to coat, shaking off any excess. Reserve the remaining spiced flour.

Heat 1 tablespoon of the oil in a heavy-based frying pan, add the lamb and cook over a high heat, stirring frequently, for 3 minutes until browned all over. Using a slotted spoon, transfer the lamb to the slow cooker.

Add the onion and garlic to the frying pan with the remaining oil, if necessary, and cook over a low heat, stirring occasionally, for 5 minutes until softened. Sprinkle in the reserved spiced flour and cook, stirring constantly, for 2 minutes, then remove the frying pan from the heat. Gradually stir in the orange juice and stock, then return the frying pan to the heat and bring to the boil, stirring constantly.

Pour the mixture over the lamb, add the cinnamon stick, red peppers, tomatoes and coriander sprigs and stir well. Cover and cook on low for 7–8 hours until the meat is tender.

Remove and discard the cinnamon stick and coriander sprigs. Serve immediately with mashed sweet potatoes and cooked green beans.

Chicken Stew

3 tbsp vegetable oil

1 large onion, thinly sliced

1 green pepper, deseeded and chopped

8 chicken portions, such as thighs and drumsticks

400 g/14 oz canned chopped tomatoes, drained

Pinch of cayenne pepper

1 tbsp Worcestershire sauce

300 ml/10 fl oz boiling chicken stock

1 tbsp cornflour

2–3 tbsp water

150 g/5½ oz frozen sweetcorn kernels, thawed

450 g/1 lb frozen broad beans, thawed

Salt

Crusty bread, to serve

Heat the oil in a large, heavy-based frying pan. Add the onion and green pepper and cook over a medium heat, stirring occasionally, for 5 minutes until the onion is softened. Using a slotted spoon, transfer the mixture to the slow cooker.

Add the chicken to the frying pan and cook, turning occasionally, for 5 minutes until golden all over. Transfer to the slow cooker and add the tomatoes. Add the cayenne pepper and season to taste with salt. Stir the Worcestershire sauce into the hot stock and pour into the slow cooker. Cover and cook on low for 6½ hours.

Mix the cornflour to a paste with the water and stir into the stew. Add the sweetcorn and broad beans, re-cover and cook on high for 30–40 minutes until the vegetables and chicken are tender and the juices run clear when a skewer is inserted into the thickest part of the meat. Transfer to warmed plates and serve with crusty bread.

Thick Beef & Baby Onion Casserole

serves 6

2 tbsp olive oil

450 g/1 lb baby onions, peeled but left whole

2 garlic cloves, halved

900 g/2 lb braising steak, cubed

½ tsp ground cinnamon

1 tsp ground cloves

1 tsp ground cumin

2 tbsp tomato purée

750 ml/1¼ pints red wine

Grated rind and juice of 1 orange

1 bay leaf

Salt and pepper

Chopped fresh flat-leaf parsley, to garnish

Boiled potatoes, to serve

Heat the oil in a heavy-based frying pan. Add the onions and garlic and cook over a medium heat, stirring frequently, for 5 minutes until softened and beginning to brown. Increase the heat to high, add the beef and cook, stirring frequently, for 5 minutes until browned all over.

Stir in the cinnamon, cloves, cumin and tomato purée and season with salt and pepper. Pour in the wine, scraping up any sediment from the base of the frying pan. Stir in the orange rind and juice, add the bay leaf and bring to the boil.

Transfer the mixture to the slow cooker, cover and cook on low for 9 hours until the beef is tender. If possible, stir the stew once during the second half of the cooking time. Remove and discard the bay leaf.

Serve the stew garnished with the parsley and accompanied by boiled potatoes.

Chicken Braised with Red Cabbage

2 tbsp vegetable oil

4 skinless chicken thighs or drumsticks, about 175 g/6 oz each

1 onion, chopped

500 g/1 lb 2 oz red cabbage, grated

2 apples, peeled, cored and chopped

12 canned or cooked chestnuts, halved (optional)

6 juniper berries (optional)

125 ml/4 fl oz red wine

Salt and pepper

Chopped fresh flat-leaf parsley, to garnish

Heat the oil in a large, heavy-based saucepan. Add the chicken and cook, turning frequently, for 5 minutes until golden on all sides. Using a slotted spoon, transfer to a plate lined with kitchen paper.

Add the onion to the pan and cook over a medium heat, stirring occasionally, until softened. Stir in the cabbage and apples and cook, stirring occasionally, for 5 minutes. Add the chestnuts and juniper berries, if using. Pour in the wine and season to taste with salt and pepper. Bring to the boil.

Spoon half the cabbage mixture into the slow cooker, then add the chicken portions and top with the remaining cabbage mixture. Cover and cook on low for 5 hours until the chicken is tender and the juices run clear when a skewer is inserted into the thickest part of the meat. Serve immediately, garnished with the chopped parsley.

Vegetarian Paella

1 litre/1¾ pints hot vegetable stock

Large pinch of saffron threads, lightly crushed

4 tbsp olive oil

1 onion, sliced

2 garlic cloves, finely chopped

1 yellow pepper, deseeded and sliced

1 red pepper, deseeded and sliced

1 large aubergine, diced

225 g/8 oz paella or risotto rice

6 tomatoes, peeled and chopped

115 g/4 oz chestnut mushrooms, sliced

115 g/4 oz green beans, halved

400 g/14 oz canned borlotti beans, drained and rinsed

Salt and pepper

Put 3 tablespoons of the hot stock into a small bowl and stir in the saffron, then leave to infuse.

Heat the oil in a large frying pan. Add the onion and garlic and cook over a low heat, stirring occasionally, for 5 minutes until softened.

Add the yellow and red peppers and aubergine to the frying pan and cook, stirring occasionally, for 5 minutes. Add the rice and cook, stirring constantly, for 1 minute until the grains are coated with oil and glistening. Pour in the remaining stock and add the tomatoes, mushrooms, green beans and borlotti beans. Stir in the saffron mixture and season to taste with salt and pepper.

Transfer the mixture to the slow cooker, cover and cook on low for 2½–3 hours until the rice is tender and the stock has been absorbed. Serve immediately.

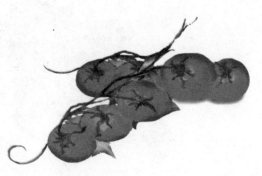

Fettuccini with Prawn & Tomato Sauce

serves 4

400 g/14 oz canned chopped tomatoes

6 tbsp tomato purée

1 garlic clove, finely chopped

2 tbsp chopped fresh parsley

500 g/1 lb 2 oz cooked, peeled large prawns

6 fresh basil leaves, torn

400 g/14 oz dried fettuccini

Salt and pepper

Put the tomatoes, tomato purée, garlic and parsley in the slow cooker and season to taste with salt and pepper. Cover and cook on low for 7 hours.

Add the prawns and basil. Re-cover and cook on high for 15 minutes.

Meanwhile, bring a large saucepan of lightly salted water to the boil. Add the pasta, bring back to the boil and cook for 10–12 minutes until tender but still firm to the bite.

Drain the pasta and tip it into a warmed serving bowl. Add the sauce and toss lightly. Serve immediately.

Chinese Beef

4 dried Chinese wood ear mushrooms

4 tbsp groundnut oil

1 kg/2 lb 4 oz topside of beef, cut into 2.5-cm/1-inch cubes

3 tbsp dark soy sauce

2 tbsp Chinese rice wine or dry sherry

1 tbsp tomato purée

2.5-cm/1-inch piece fresh ginger, very finely chopped

2 garlic cloves, very finely chopped

2 tbsp soft light brown sugar

1 tsp Chinese five-spice powder

700 ml/1¼ pints beef stock

280 g/10 oz carrots, thinly sliced diagonally

Cooked egg noodles, to serve

Put the mushrooms into a heatproof bowl and pour in warm water to cover. Set aside to soak for 20 minutes.

Meanwhile, heat the oil in a large saucepan. Add the beef, in batches, and cook over a medium heat, stirring frequently, for 8–10 minutes until evenly browned. Remove with a slotted spoon and drain on kitchen paper.

Drain the mushrooms, discarding the soaking water, and gently squeeze out any excess liquid. Cut off and discard the stalks, slice the caps and put them into a bowl. Add the soy sauce, rice wine, tomato purée, ginger, garlic, sugar, five-spice powder and stock and mix well.

When all the meat has been browned, wipe out the pan with kitchen paper. Return the meat to the pan, stir in the mushroom mixture and bring to the boil.

Transfer the mixture to the slow cooker, cover and cook on low for 8 hours until the meat is tender. Stir in the carrots, re-cover and cook on high for a further 45–60 minutes until the carrots are tender. Serve immediately with egg noodles.

Pork & Vegetable Ragout

serves 4

450 g/1 lb lean, boneless pork

1½ tbsp plain flour

1 tsp ground coriander

1 tsp ground cumin

1½ tsp ground cinnamon

1 tbsp olive oil

1 onion, chopped

400 g/14 oz canned chopped tomatoes

2 tbsp tomato purée

300 ml/10 fl oz chicken stock

225 g/8 oz carrots, chopped

350 g/12 oz butternut or acorn squash, peeled, deseeded and chopped

225 g/8 oz leeks, trimmed, blanched, drained and sliced

115 g/4 oz okra, trimmed and sliced

Salt and pepper

Fresh flat-leaf parsley sprigs, to garnish

Cooked couscous, to serve

Trim off any visible fat from the pork and cut the flesh into thin strips about 5 cm/2 inches long. Combine the flour, coriander, cumin and cinnamon in a shallow dish, add the pork strips and toss well to coat. Shake off the excess and reserve the remaining spiced flour.

Heat the oil in a heavy-based frying pan. Add the onion and cook over a low heat, stirring occasionally, for 5 minutes until softened. Add the pork strips, increase the heat to high and cook, stirring frequently, for 5 minutes until browned all over. Sprinkle in the reserved spiced flour and cook, stirring constantly, for 2 minutes, then remove the frying pan from the heat.

Gradually stir in the tomatoes. Combine the tomato purée with the stock in a jug, then gradually stir the mixture into the frying pan. Add the carrots, return the frying pan to the heat and bring to the boil, stirring constantly.

Transfer to the slow cooker, stir in the squash, leeks and okra and season to taste with salt and pepper. Cover and cook on low for 5–6 hours until the meat and vegetables are tender and cooked through. Garnish with parsley sprigs and serve with couscous.

Spring Vegetable Stew

serves 4

225 g/8 oz dried
cannellini beans,
soaked in cold water
overnight or for at least
5 hours, drained and
rinsed

2 tbsp olive oil

4–8 baby onions, halved

2 celery sticks, cut into
5-mm/¼-inch slices

12 baby carrots, halved
if large

300 g/10½ oz new
potatoes, halved

1–1.2 litres/1¾–2 pints
vegetable stock

1 bouquet garni

2 tbsp light soy sauce

125 g/4½ oz baby corn

100 g/3½ oz shelled
broad beans, thawed if
frozen

250 g/9 oz Savoy
cabbage, shredded

1½ tbsp cornflour

3 tbsp water

Salt and pepper

85 g/3 oz freshly grated
Parmesan cheese,
to serve

Boil the cannellini beans in a saucepan of rapidly boiling water for 10 minutes, drain and rinse well with fresh water.

Heat the oil in a saucepan. Add the onions, celery, carrots and potatoes and cook over a low heat, stirring frequently, for 5–8 minutes until softened. Add the stock, cannellini beans, bouquet garni and soy sauce. Bring to the boil, then transfer the mixture to the slow cooker. Add the baby corn, broad beans and cabbage, season to taste with salt and pepper and stir well. Cover and cook on high for 3–4 hours until the vegetables are tender.

Remove and discard the bouquet garni. Mix the cornflour and water to a paste in a jug, then stir into the stew. Re-cover and cook on high for 15 minutes until thickened. Serve the stew with the Parmesan on the side.

Lamb Shanks with Olives

1½ tbsp plain flour

4 lamb shanks

2 tbsp olive oil

1 onion, sliced

2 garlic cloves, finely chopped

2 tsp sweet paprika

400 g/14 oz canned chopped tomatoes

2 tbsp tomato purée

2 carrots, sliced

2 tsp sugar

225 ml/8 fl oz red wine

5-cm/2-inch cinnamon stick

2 fresh rosemary sprigs

115 g/4 oz stoned black olives

2 tbsp lemon juice

2 tbsp chopped fresh mint, plus extra leaves to garnish

Salt and pepper

Put the flour into a plastic food bag and season to taste with salt and pepper. Add the lamb shanks, hold the top securely and shake well to coat.

Heat the oil in a large, heavy-based saucepan. Add the lamb shanks and cook over a medium heat, turning frequently, for 6–8 minutes until evenly browned. Transfer to a plate and set aside.

Add the onion and garlic to the pan and cook, stirring frequently, for 5 minutes until softened. Stir in the paprika and cook for 1 minute. Add the tomatoes, tomato purée, carrots, sugar, wine, cinnamon stick and rosemary sprigs and bring to the boil.

Transfer the mixture to the slow cooker and add the lamb shanks. Cover and cook on low for 8 hours until the lamb is very tender.

Add the olives, lemon juice and chopped mint to the slow cooker. Re-cover and cook on high for 30 minutes. Remove and discard the rosemary sprigs and cinnamon stick. Garnish with mint leaves and serve immediately.

Chilli Chicken

2 tbsp sunflower oil

6 chicken portions

2 onions, chopped

2 garlic cloves, chopped

1 fresh chilli, deseeded and chopped

6 tomatoes, peeled and chopped

2 tsp sweet paprika

1 bay leaf

225 ml/8 fl oz hot chicken stock

Salt and pepper

Heat the oil in a heavy-based frying pan. Add the chicken and cook over a medium heat, turning occasionally, for about 10 minutes until browned.

Transfer the chicken to the slow cooker and add the onions, garlic, chilli and tomatoes. Sprinkle in the paprika, add the bay leaf and pour in the stock. Season to taste with salt and pepper.

Stir well, cover and cook on low for 6 hours until the chicken is tender and the juices run clear when a skewer is inserted into the thickest part of the meat. Remove and discard the bay leaf. Serve immediately.

Pork with Almonds

serves 4

2 tbsp sunflower oil

2 onions, chopped

2 garlic cloves, finely chopped

5-cm/2-inch cinnamon stick

3 cloves

115 g/4 oz ground almonds

750 g/1 lb 10 oz boneless pork, cut into 2.5-cm/1-inch cubes

4 tomatoes, peeled and chopped

2 tbsp capers

115 g/4 oz stoned green olives

3 pickled jalapeño chillies, drained, deseeded and cut into rings

350 ml/12 fl oz chicken stock

Salt and pepper

Fresh coriander sprigs, to garnish

Heat half the oil in a large, heavy-based frying pan. Add the onions and cook over a low heat, stirring occasionally, for 5 minutes until softened. Add the garlic, cinnamon stick, cloves and ground almonds and cook, stirring frequently, for 8–10 minutes. Take care not to burn the almonds.

Remove and discard the spices and transfer the mixture to a food processor. Process to a smooth purée.

Rinse out the frying pan and return to the heat. Heat the remaining oil, then add the pork, in batches if necessary. Cook over a medium heat, stirring frequently, for 5–10 minutes until browned all over. Return all the pork to the frying pan and add the almond purée, tomatoes, capers, olives, chillies and stock. Bring to the boil, then transfer to the slow cooker.

Season to taste with salt and pepper and mix well. Cover and cook on low for 5 hours. To serve, transfer to warmed plates and garnish with coriander sprigs.

3

Salads & Side Dishes

Roast Summer Vegetables

serves 4

2 tbsp olive oil

1 fennel bulb, cut into wedges

2 red onions, cut into wedges

2 beef tomatoes, cut into wedges

1 aubergine, thickly sliced

2 courgettes, thickly sliced

1 yellow pepper, deseeded and cut into chunks

1 red pepper, deseeded and cut into chunks

1 orange pepper, deseeded and cut into chunks

4 garlic cloves

4 fresh rosemary sprigs

Pepper

Crusty bread, to serve (optional)

Preheat the oven to 200°C/400°F/Gas Mark 6. Brush an ovenproof dish with a little of the oil. Arrange the fennel, onions, tomatoes, aubergine, courgettes and yellow, red and orange peppers in the dish and tuck the garlic cloves and rosemary sprigs among them. Drizzle with the remaining oil and season to taste with pepper.

Roast the vegetables in the preheated oven for 10 minutes. Turn the vegetables over, return the dish to the oven and roast for a further 10–15 minutes or until the vegetables are tender and beginning to turn golden brown.

Serve the vegetables straight from the dish or transfer to a warmed serving platter. Serve immediately with crusty bread, if using, to soak up the juices.

Mozzarella Cheese & Tomato Salad

serves 4

450 g/1 lb cherry tomatoes

4 spring onions

125 ml/4 fl oz extra virgin olive oil

2 tbsp best-quality balsamic vinegar

175 g/6 oz buffalo mozzarella cheese, cut into cubes

25 g/1 oz fresh flat-leaf parsley

25 g/1 oz fresh basil leaves

Salt and pepper

Using a sharp knife, cut the tomatoes in half and put in a large bowl. Trim the spring onions, finely chop the green and white parts and add to the bowl.

Pour in the oil and vinegar and use your hands to toss together. Season with salt and pepper, add the mozzarella cheese and toss again. Cover and chill for 4 hours.

Remove the salad from the refrigerator 10 minutes before serving. Finely chop the parsley and add to the salad. Tear the basil leaves over the salad and toss all the ingredients together again. Adjust the seasoning and serve.

Courgette Fritters

makes 16-30

40 g/1½ oz self-raising flour

2 eggs, beaten

4 tbsp milk

2 courgettes

2 tbsp chopped fresh thyme

1 tbsp oil

Salt and pepper

Sift the flour into a large bowl and make a well in the centre. Add the eggs to the well and, using a wooden spoon, gradually draw in the flour.

Slowly add the milk to the mixture, stirring continuously to form a thick mixture.

Grate the courgettes over kitchen paper placed in a bowl to absorb some of the juices.

Add the courgettes, thyme and salt and pepper to taste to the flour mixture and mix thoroughly.

Heat the oil in a large, heavy-based frying pan. Taking a tablespoon of the mixture for a medium-sized fritter or ½ tablespoon for a smaller fritter, spoon the mixture into the hot oil and cook, in batches, for 3–4 minutes on each side.

Remove the fritters with a slotted spoon and drain thoroughly on kitchen paper. Keep each batch of fritters warm in the oven while making the rest. Transfer to warmed serving plates and serve hot.

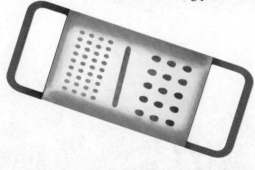

Boston Baked Beans

serves 10

450 g/1 lb dried haricot beans

1.5 litres/2½ pints water

Pinch of bicarbonate of soda

1 bay leaf

6 bacon rashers, cut into 1-cm/½-inch pieces

1 onion, diced

5 tbsp treacle

4 tbsp muscovado sugar

1 tsp mustard powder

1½ tsp salt, or to taste

½ tsp pepper

Preheat the oven to 150°C/300°F/Gas Mark 2.

Place the beans and water in a large saucepan or casserole and leave to soak overnight. Add the bicarbonate of soda and bay leaf and bring to the boil. Reduce the heat to medium and simmer for 10 minutes. Drain into a colander set over a large bowl and reserve the liquid.

Transfer the drained beans into a casserole and add the rest of the ingredients. Stir until combined. Add enough of the reserved cooking liquid to just barely cover the beans.

Cover the casserole tightly and place in the preheated oven for 1 hour. Uncover and check the liquid level. Add some more of the reserved liquid if the beans are getting too dry. Cover and cook for a further hour or until tender. Uncover and test the beans – they should be starting to get tender, but if they're still firm, cover and cook a bit longer, adding more liquid if they're getting too dry.

When just tender, turn the oven temperature up to 180°C/350°F/Gas Mark 4 and continue to cook, uncovered, for a further 30 minutes to reduce the liquid and create a thick, syrupy consistency. Serve hot or at room temperature.

Creamed Spinach

115 g/4 oz unsalted butter

650 g/1 lb 7 oz baby spinach leaves, tough stalks removed

½ onion, finely diced

40 g/1½ oz plain flour

3 garlic cloves, very finely chopped

350 ml/12 fl oz cold milk

Pinch of freshly grated nutmeg

Salt and pepper

Put a large saucepan over a high heat. Add 15 g/½ oz of the butter and, as soon as it melts, add all the spinach and cover quickly. Leave for 1 minute, uncover and continue cooking, stirring the spinach with a long wooden spoon, until just barely wilted. Transfer to a colander to drain.

When the spinach is cool enough to handle, squeeze as much liquid out as possible and roughly chop. Press between kitchen paper to draw out the last of the water and reserve until needed.

Melt the remaining butter in a saucepan over a medium heat. Add the onion and cook for about 5 minutes or until translucent. Whisk in the flour and cook for 3 minutes, stirring. Add the garlic and cook for 1 minute. Pour in the cold milk, whisking constantly, and cook until it comes to a simmer. Reduce the heat to low and simmer for a further 5 minutes. The sauce will thicken as it cooks.

Season the sauce with the nutmeg and salt and pepper to taste. Add the spinach and stir to combine. The dish is ready to serve as soon as the spinach is heated through. Taste and adjust the seasoning before serving.

Perfect Mashed Potatoes

900 g/2 lb potatoes, such as Desiree, Estima or King Edward

55 g/2 oz butter

3 tbsp milk

Salt and pepper

Peel the potatoes, placing them in cold water as you prepare the others to prevent them from going brown.

Cut the potatoes into even-sized chunks and cook in a large saucepan of boiling salted water over a medium heat, covered, for 20–25 minutes until they are tender. Test with the point of a knife, but do make sure you test right to the middle to avoid lumps.

Remove the pan from the heat and drain the potatoes. Return the potatoes to the hot pan and mash with a potato masher until smooth.

Add the butter and continue to mash until it is all mixed in, then add the milk.

Taste the mash and season with salt and pepper as necessary. Serve immediately.

Variations: For herb mash, mix in 3 tablespoons of chopped fresh parsley, thyme or mint. For mustard or horseradish mash, mix in 2 tablespoons of wholegrain mustard or horseradish sauce. For pesto mash, stir in 4 tablespoons of fresh pesto. For nutmeg mash, grate half a nutmeg into the mash and add 125 ml/4 fl oz natural yogurt. To make creamed potatoes, add 125 ml/4 fl oz crème fraîche or soured cream and 2 tablespoons of snipped fresh chives.

Macaroni Salad

450 g/1 lb dried elbow macaroni

Salt

For the dressing

350 g/12 oz mayonnaise

115 g/4 oz soured cream

2 tbsp cider vinegar

1 tbsp Dijon mustard

1 tsp sugar

55 g/2 oz celery, finely diced

40 g/1½ oz red onion, finely chopped

70 g/2½ oz sweet gerkin relish

35 g/1¼ oz carrot, finely grated

2 tbsp finely diced red pepper

15 g/½ oz fresh parsley, chopped

½ tsp pepper

1½ tsp salt, or to taste

Bring a large saucepan of lightly salted water to the boil. Add the pasta, bring back to the boil and cook for 8–10 minutes until tender but still firm to the bite. Drain, rinse under cold running water and drain again.

Whisk together the dressing ingredients in a large mixing bowl. Add the drained pasta and toss to combine thoroughly. Cover and leave to chill in the refrigerator for at least 2 hours before serving.

Ratatouille

serves 8

1 red pepper, deseeded and quartered

1 orange pepper, deseeded and quartered

1 green pepper, deseeded and quartered

550 g/1 lb 4 oz aubergine, thickly sliced

2 tbsp olive oil, plus extra for brushing

2 large onions, sliced

3 garlic cloves, finely chopped

3 courgettes, thickly sliced

5–6 tomatoes, peeled, deseeded and chopped

1½ tsp mixed dried herbs

2 bay leaves

Salt and pepper

Crusty bread, to serve

Preheat the grill. Put the red, orange and green pepper quarters, skin-side up, on a baking tray and place under the preheated grill until the skins are charred and blistered. Remove with tongs, put them into a plastic bag, tie the top and let cool. Meanwhile, spread out the aubergine slices on the baking tray, brush with oil and grill for 5 minutes until lightly browned. Turn, brush with oil and grill for a further 5 minutes until lightly browned. Remove with tongs.

Remove the peppers from the bag and peel off the skins. Remove and discard the seeds and membranes and cut the flesh into strips. Dice the aubergine slices.

Heat the oil in a large saucepan. Add the onions and cook over a low heat, stirring occasionally, for 8–10 minutes until lightly browned. Add the garlic and courgettes, and cook, stirring occasionally, for a further 10 minutes.

Stir in the peppers, aubergines, tomatoes, mixed dried herbs and bay leaves. Season to taste with salt and pepper, then cover and simmer over a very low heat, stirring occasionally, for 25 minutes. Remove the lid and simmer, stirring occasionally, for a further 25–35 minutes until all the vegetables are tender.

Remove and discard the bay leaves. Serve the ratatouille immediately if serving hot, or leave to cool if serving at room temperature, accompanied by crusty bread.

Cheese & Chive Bread

serves 8

250 g/9 oz self-raising flour

1 tsp salt

1 tsp mustard powder

115 g/4 oz mature Cheddar cheese, grated

2 tbsp snipped fresh chives

1 egg, beaten

25 g/1 oz butter, melted, plus extra for greasing

150 ml/5 fl oz milk

Preheat the oven to 190°C/375°F/Gas Mark 5. Grease a 23-cm/9-inch square cake tin and line the base with baking paper.

Sift the flour, salt and mustard powder into a large mixing bowl.

Reserve 3 tablespoons of the grated cheese for sprinkling over the top of the loaf before baking in the oven. Stir the remaining cheese into the bowl, together with the chives. Mix well.

Add the beaten egg, melted butter and milk and stir the mixture thoroughly.

Pour the mixture into the prepared pan and spread with a knife. Sprinkle with the reserved grated cheese. Bake in the preheated oven for about 30 minutes.

Leave the bread to cool slightly in the tin. Turn out onto a wire rack to cool further before serving. Cut into triangles to serve.

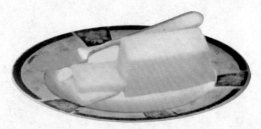

Rocket & Parmesan Salad with Pine Nuts

serves 4

2 handfuls of rocket
leaves

1 small fennel bulb

5 tbsp olive oil

2 tbsp balsamic vinegar

50 g/1¾ oz Parmesan
cheese

35 g/1¼ oz pine nuts

Salt and pepper

Wash the rocket, discarding any wilted leaves and tough stalks, and pat dry. Divide between 4 serving plates. Halve the fennel bulb and slice it finely. Arrange the sliced fennel over the rocket.

Whisk together the oil and vinegar with salt and pepper to taste. Drizzle a little of the dressing over each serving. Shave the Parmesan cheese thinly using a knife or vegetable peeler.

Toast the pine nuts in a dry frying pan until golden brown. Top the salad with the Parmesan cheese shavings and toasted pine nuts. Serve immediately.

Macaroni Cheese

serves 6

85 g/3 oz butter, plus extra for greasing

85 g/3 oz onion, very finely chopped

3 tbsp plain flour

700 ml/1¼ pints cold milk

½ tsp chopped fresh thyme leaves

Small pinch of freshly grated nutmeg

Pinch of cayenne pepper

225 g/8 oz dried elbow macaroni

225 g/8 oz Cheddar cheese, grated

115 g/4 oz Gruyère cheese, grated

70 g/2½ oz dried breadcrumbs

Salt and pepper

Preheat the oven to 180°C/350°F/Gas Mark 4. Lightly grease a 23 x 33-cm/9 x 13-inch baking dish.

Melt 55 g/2 oz of the butter in a saucepan over a medium heat. Sauté the onions in the butter for 4–5 minutes until translucent. Do not brown. Stir in the flour and cook for 2 minutes. Whisk in the cold milk and cook, stirring, until the mixture comes to a simmer and thickens slightly. Turn off the heat and stir in the thyme, nutmeg, cayenne pepper and salt and pepper to taste. Set aside.

Cook the macaroni in a large saucepan of salted boiling water for 1 minute less than the packet instructions. Drain well and transfer to a large mixing bowl. Add the white sauce and the cheeses and fold with a spatula until thoroughly combined.

Transfer to the prepared baking dish. Melt the remaining butter and mix with the breadcrumbs. Scatter evenly over the top of the casserole. Bake in the preheated oven for 40–45 minutes or until bubbly and golden brown. Cover loosely with foil towards the end of the cooking if the top is getting too brown for your liking.

Baked Acorn Squash

serves 4

2 acorn squash
2 tbsp orange juice
1 tbsp soft brown sugar
25 g/1 oz unsalted butter
2 tbsp maple syrup
Salt and pepper

Preheat the oven to 200°C/400°F/Gas Mark 6.

Cut the acorn squash in half lengthways and scoop the seeds and strings out of the cavity. Carefully score the inside of each squash with a sharp knife, making 3 mm/⅛ inch deep cuts about 1 cm/½ inch apart. Brush each half with the orange juice, sprinkle generously with salt and bake in the preheated oven for 30 minutes.

In a small saucepan, combine the brown sugar, butter, maple syrup and pepper to taste. Bring to the boil, stir and cook for 1 minute. Reserve.

Remove the squash from the oven and spoon off any liquid that has accumulated in the cavities. Brush the glaze evenly over each and bake for a further 40 minutes or until tender and caramelized on the edges. For an extra nice glaze, baste the squash with the syrup that collects in the cavity a few times while it's baking. Allow to stand for 15 minutes before serving.

Braised Red Cabbage & Apples

serves 6

1 tsp caraway seeds

1 tbsp vegetable oil

1 red onion, halved and thinly sliced

2 tbsp soft brown sugar

1 small red cabbage, shredded

2 apples, peeled and thinly sliced

2 tbsp red wine

125 ml/4 fl oz apple juice

2 tbsp cider vinegar

1 tsp lemon juice

Salt and pepper

Dry roast the caraway seeds in a saucepan over a medium heat for about 1 minute until they start to give off an aroma.

Heat the oil in a large saucepan over a medium heat, add the onion and sauté for 5 minutes until it becomes translucent. Add the brown sugar, stir and add the cabbage and apples. Stir for a few minutes until the cabbage wilts. Pour in the red wine, apple juice and vinegar. Add the toasted caraway seeds and salt and pepper to taste. Bring the mixture to the boil, then lower to a simmer, add the lemon juice and cook, covered, for 30 minutes.

Note: Braised cabbage is wonderful served with chicken, meat or pork dishes.

Bread Rolls

makes 16

4 tbsp lukewarm water

7-g/¼-oz sachet easy-blend dried yeast

225 ml/8 fl oz milk

40 g/1½ oz unsalted butter, at room temperature

1 tbsp sugar

1 tbsp clear honey

¾ tsp salt

375 g/13 oz plain white flour, plus extra for dusting

1 tsp vegetable oil

Combine the water and yeast in a large bowl. Whisk until dissolved and set aside. Combine the milk, butter, sugar, honey and salt in another non-metallic bowl. Microwave for 1 minute or until the milk is just warm. Set aside until the butter is melted.

Add the flour to the bowl containing the water and yeast, followed by the milk mixture. Stir until a sticky dough forms. Turn the dough out onto a well-floured work surface. Knead the dough for about 6 minutes, adding enough flour to prevent the dough from sticking to the surface or your hands. Grease a large bowl with the oil. Place the dough into the bowl, cover with a clean tea towel and leave to rise in a warm place for about 1½ hours until it doubles in size.

Knock back the dough and turn it out onto a lightly floured surface. Shape into a square and cut into 16 equal-sized pieces. Roll each piece into a ball. Line a 46 x 33-cm/18 x 13-inch baking tray with a silicone baking sheet. Place each ball, seam-side down, about 5 cm/2 inches apart on the baking tray. Put a teaspoon of flour in a fine mesh sieve and tap to dust the top of each roll with a little flour. Allow to rise for 40 minutes. Meanwhile, preheat the oven to 180°C/350°F/Gas Mark 4.

Bake in the centre of the preheated oven for about 25 minutes until golden brown. Remove and leave to cool on a wire rack for 20 minutes before serving.

Dauphinoise Potatoes

serves 8

Butter, for greasing

2 kg/4 lb 8 oz potatoes, such as Desiree, thinly sliced

55 g/2 oz Gruyère or Cheddar cheese, grated

Salt and black pepper

For the white sauce

15 g/½ oz butter

1 tbsp plain flour

225 ml/8 fl oz single cream

475 ml/16 fl oz milk

1 tsp salt

Pinch of freshly grated nutmeg

Pinch of white pepper

4 fresh thyme sprigs

2 garlic cloves, finely chopped

Preheat the oven to 190°C/375°F/Gas Mark 5. Grease a 38 x 25-cm/15 x 10-inch baking dish.

To make the sauce, melt the butter in a saucepan over a medium heat. Stir in the flour and cook, stirring constantly, for 2 minutes. Whisk in the cream and milk and bring to a simmer. Add the salt, nutmeg, white pepper, thyme and garlic. Reduce the heat to low and simmer for 5 minutes. Remove and discard the thyme sprigs.

Layer half the potatoes in the prepared baking dish. Season generously with salt and black pepper. Top with half the sauce and scatter over half the cheese. Repeat with the remaining potatoes, sauce and cheese.

Bake in the preheated oven for about 1 hour or until the top is browned and the potatoes are tender. Leave to rest for 15 minutes before serving.

Caesar Salad with Garlic Croûtons

For the dressing

2 eggs, at room temperature

2 large garlic cloves, finely chopped

3 whole anchovy fillets

175 g/6 oz mayonnaise

55 g/2 oz finely grated Parmesan cheese

5 tbsp olive oil

4 tbsp lemon juice

1 tbsp cold water

1 tsp pepper, or to taste

Salt, to taste

For the salad

6 hearts of cos lettuce, torn or cut into 5-cm/ 2-inch pieces, washed and dried thoroughly

125 g/4½ oz croûtons

85 g/3 oz Parmesan cheese shavings, or to taste

Pepper

For the dressing, place the eggs in a small saucepan. Pour in boiling water until the eggs are covered. Leave for 1 minute, then drain and run under cold water until the eggs are cool enough to be handled. When cool, separate the eggs, removing and reserving the yolks. The whites aren't required for this recipe.

Add the rest of the dressing ingredients to a blender along with the egg yolks. Blend until smooth. Refrigerate until needed.

For the salad, combine the lettuce, croûtons and 175 ml/ 6 fl oz of the dressing in a large mixing bowl. Toss with tongs until the lettuce is completely coated with dressing. Divide between chilled plates and top with the Parmesan shavings and pepper to taste. Serve immediately with extra dressing on the side.

Cheese & Ham Loaf

makes 1 loaf

200 g/7 oz self-raising flour

1 tsp salt

2 tsp baking powder

1 tsp paprika

85 g/3 oz butter, diced, plus extra for greasing

175 g/6 oz mature Cheddar cheese, grated

70 g/2½ oz smoked ham, chopped

2 eggs, lightly beaten

5 tbsp milk

Preheat the oven to 180°C/350°F/Gas Mark 4. Grease a 450-g/1-lb loaf tin with a little butter and line the base with baking paper.

Sift the flour, salt, baking powder and paprika into a large mixing bowl. Rub in the butter with your fingertips until the mixture resembles fine breadcrumbs. Stir in the cheese and ham. Add the beaten eggs and milk to the dry ingredients in the bowl and mix well.

Spoon the mixture into the prepared tin. Bake in the preheated oven for about 1 hour or until the loaf is well risen.

Leave the bread to cool in the tin, then turn out and transfer to a wire rack to cool completely. Cut the bread into thick slices to serve.

Green Bean Casserole

650 g/1 lb 7 oz green beans, cut into short lengths

350 ml/12 fl oz single cream

125 ml/4 fl oz chicken stock

1 garlic clove, finely chopped

½ tsp salt

¼ tsp pepper

Pinch of freshly grated nutmeg

2 onions, sliced into rings and sautéed

Preheat the oven to 190°C/375°F/Gas Mark 5.

Bring a large saucepan of water to the boil. Blanch the beans in the boiling water for 5 minutes. Drain very well and reserve.

Put the cream, stock, garlic, salt, pepper and nutmeg in a small saucepan. Place over a medium heat and cook, stirring occasionally, until the mixture comes to a simmer. Remove from the heat and reserve.

Spread half the sautéed onions in the base of a 2-litre/3½-pint casserole. Spread the beans evenly over the onions. Pour over the cream mixture. Use a fork to press the beans down into the cream. Top with the remaining onions and use a fork to flatten the top, pressing down firmly.

Bake in the preheated oven for 25–30 minutes or until the beans are very tender and the casserole is browned and bubbling. Remove from the oven and leave to rest for 15 minutes before serving.

Waldorf Salad

serves 4

85 g/3 oz walnut halves

5 tbsp mayonnaise

2 tbsp lemon juice

1 tbsp natural yogurt

½ tsp salt

Pinch of pepper

3 apples, cored and cut into 2.5-cm/1-inch chunks

150 g/5½ oz green or red seedless grapes, halved

100 g/3½ oz celery, sliced about 5 mm/ ¼ inch thick

1 small head of Little Gem lettuce

Preheat the oven to 180°C/350°F/Gas Mark 4.

Arrange the walnuts on a baking tray and bake in the preheated oven for 8 minutes. Leave to cool on a chopping board, then roughly chop and set aside.

Place the mayonnaise, lemon juice, yogurt, salt and pepper in a large mixing bowl. Whisk to combine thoroughly. Use a palette knife to fold in the apples, grapes, celery and walnuts. Mix until evenly coated with the dressing.

Arrange a few lettuce leaves on each plate and spoon the mayonnaise mixture over the top. Serve immediately.

Tip: Try using 3 different varieties of apple for an even more interesting salad.

Roast Pepper Salad

serves 4

4 large mixed red, green and yellow peppers

4 tbsp olive oil

1 large red onion, sliced

2 garlic cloves, crushed

4 tomatoes, peeled and chopped

Pinch of sugar

1 tsp lemon juice

Salt and pepper

Preheat the grill to high. Halve the peppers and remove the seeds and stalks.

Place the peppers, skin-side up, under the preheated grill. Cook until the skins have blistered and blackened. Rinse under cold water and remove and discard the skins, then slice the flesh into thin strips.

Heat the oil in a frying pan and sauté the onion and garlic until softened. Add the peppers and tomatoes and sauté over a low heat for 10 minutes.

Remove from the heat, add the sugar and lemon juice and season to taste with salt and pepper. Serve immediately or leave to cool (the flavours will develop as the salad cools).

Sweetcorn & Butter Beans with Mixed Vegetables

serves 8

1 tbsp olive oil

7 g/¼ oz butter

½ onion, diced

3 garlic cloves, finely chopped

1 jalapeño or other small hot chilli pepper, sliced

½ red pepper, deseeded and diced

85 g/3 oz tomatoes, chopped

100 g/3½ oz green beans, cut into 1-cm/½-inch lengths

225 g/8 oz fresh or frozen sweetcorn kernels

200 g/7 oz canned butter beans, drained and rinsed

55 g/2 oz courgette, diced

½ tsp ground cumin

Pinch of cayenne pepper

4 tbsp water, plus extra if needed

Salt and pepper

Place a large frying pan over a medium heat and add the oil and butter. When the butter foams up, add the onion and a big pinch of salt. Sauté for about 5 minutes or until the onion begins to soften and turn golden.

Add the garlic, chilli and red pepper and sauté for 3 minutes. Add the rest of the ingredients and cook, stirring occasionally, until the vegetables are tender. Add more water if the mixture gets too dry.

When done, taste and adjust the seasoning, adding salt and pepper if needed. Serve immediately.

Turkey Couscous Salad

serves 4

250 g/9 oz couscous

5 tbsp olive oil

3 tbsp red wine vinegar

350 g/12 oz turkey
breast fillet, cubed

1 tsp harissa paste

175 g/6 oz courgette,
diced

1 onion, chopped

60 g/2¼ oz ready-to-eat
dried apricots, chopped

2 tbsp toasted pine nuts

2 tbsp chopped fresh
coriander, plus extra
to garnish

Salt and pepper

Put the couscous into a large heatproof bowl. Pour in enough boiling water to cover. Stir well, cover and leave to soak for about 5 minutes until all the liquid has been absorbed. Use a fork to separate the grains and stir in 3 tablespoons of the oil and the vinegar. Season with plenty of salt and pepper.

Heat the remaining oil in a large frying pan and add the turkey and harissa paste. Cook, turning frequently, for 3 minutes until the turkey is no longer pink. Add the courgette and onion to the pan and cook, stirring occasionally, for a further 10–12 minutes until the turkey and vegetables are golden brown and tender.

Stir the turkey and vegetables into the couscous with the apricots and pine nuts. Leave to cool for 10 minutes, then stir in the chopped coriander and adjust the seasoning to taste. Transfer to serving bowls, garnish with coriander and serve immediately.

Polenta Balls

makes 36

250 g/9 oz polenta

60 g/2¼ oz plain flour, sifted

1 small onion, finely chopped

1 tbsp granulated sugar

2 tsp baking powder

½ tsp salt

175 ml/6 fl oz milk

1 egg, beaten

Vegetable oil, for deep-frying

Stir the polenta, flour, onion, sugar, baking powder and salt together in a bowl and make a well in the centre.

Beat the milk and egg together in a jug, then pour into the dry ingredients and stir until a thick mixture forms.

Heat enough oil for deep-frying in a large saucepan or deep-fryer to 180–190°C/350–375°F or until a cube of bread browns in 30 seconds.

Drop in as many teaspoonsful of the mixture as will fit without overcrowding the pan and cook, stirring constantly, until the polenta balls puff up and turn golden.

Remove the polenta balls from the oil with a slotted spoon and drain on kitchen paper. Reheat the oil if necessary and cook the remaining mixture. Serve hot.

Chicken & Avocado Salad

serves 4

8 streaky bacon rashers

4 large handfuls of mixed baby salad leaves, or other lettuce, torn into bite-sized pieces

3 hard-boiled eggs, shelled and chopped

550 g/1 lb 4 oz cooked chicken, cubed

2 avocados, peeled, stoned and cubed

150 g/5½ oz cherry tomatoes, halved

55 g/2 oz Roquefort cheese, crumbled

½ tsp Dijon mustard

4 tbsp red wine vinegar

1 tsp Worcestershire sauce

1 garlic clove, crushed into a paste

¼ tsp salt

¼ tsp pepper

5 tbsp olive oil

Cook the bacon until crisp, then drain on kitchen paper. When cool enough to handle, crumble and set aside.

Line 4 shallow bowls with the salad leaves. Arrange the eggs, bacon, chicken, avocados, tomatoes and Roquefort cheese on top of the lettuce.

In a bowl, whisk together the mustard, vinegar, Worcestershire sauce, garlic, salt and pepper. Slowly drizzle in the oil, whisking constantly, to form the dressing.

Drizzle the dressing evenly over the salad and serve immediately.

Baked Sweetcorn Puddings

Butter, for greasing

450 g/1 lb sweetcorn kernels, thawed if frozen

350 ml/12 fl oz double cream

125 ml/4 fl oz milk

1¼ tsp salt

Pinch of cayenne pepper

3 egg yolks

4 eggs

Preheat the oven to 160°C/325°F/Gas Mark 3. Grease 8 x 175-g/6-oz ramekins with butter.

Place the sweetcorn, cream, milk, salt and cayenne pepper in a saucepan. Bring to a simmer over a medium heat. Turn off the heat and leave to cool slightly. Carefully pour into a blender and purée until very smooth. Set aside.

Put the egg yolks and eggs into a mixing bowl and whisk for 30 seconds. Slowly, a little at a time, stir in the warm sweetcorn mixture. When everything is combined, ladle the mixture into the prepared ramekins.

Fill a roasting tin with 2.5 cm/1 inch of hot water and place the filled ramekins in it. Bake in the preheated oven for 35 minutes or until just set. Remove from the roasting tin and leave to cool for 15 minutes before serving. Serve in the ramekins, or run a thin knife around the inside of each ramekin and turn out onto a plate.

Cajun Chicken Salad

serves 4

4 skinless, boneless chicken breasts

4 tsp Cajun seasoning

2 tsp vegetable oil

1 ripe mango, peeled, stoned and cut into thick slices

200 g/7 oz mixed salad leaves

1 red onion, halved and thinly sliced

200 g/7 oz cooked beetroot, diced

55 g/2 oz radishes, sliced

55 g/2 oz walnut halves

2 tbsp sesame seeds

For the dressing

4 tbsp walnut oil

1–2 tsp wholegrain mustard

1 tbsp lemon juice

Salt and pepper

Make 3 diagonal slashes across each chicken breast. Put the chicken into a shallow dish and sprinkle all over with the Cajun seasoning. Cover and leave to chill for at least 30 minutes.

When ready to cook, brush a griddle pan with the vegetable oil. Heat over a high heat until very hot and a few drops of water sprinkled into the pan sizzle immediately. Add the chicken and cook for 7–8 minutes on each side or until the juices run clear when a skewer is inserted into the thickest part of the meat. Remove the chicken from the pan and set aside.

Add the mango slices to the pan and cook for 2 minutes on each side. Remove and set aside.

Meanwhile, arrange the salad leaves on 4 serving plates and sprinkle over the onion, beetroot, radishes and walnut halves.

To make the dressing, put the walnut oil, mustard, lemon juice and salt and pepper to taste in a screw-top jar and shake until well blended. Pour over the salad and sprinkle with the sesame seeds.

Cut the chicken into thick slices. Arrange the chicken and mango slices on top of the salad and serve immediately.

Cheesy Broccoli Bake

serves 6

900 g/2 lb broccoli, cut into 5-cm/2-inch florets

50 g/1¾ oz dried breadcrumbs

25 g/1 oz butter, melted, plus extra for greasing

2 tbsp grated Parmesan cheese

For the cheese sauce

55 g/2 oz butter

35 g/1¼ oz flour

475 ml/16 fl oz cold milk

Pinch of freshly grated nutmeg

Pinch of cayenne pepper

1 tsp chopped fresh thyme leaves

115 g/4 oz extra-mature Cheddar cheese, grated

½ tsp salt, or to taste

Preheat the oven to 190°C/375°F/Gas Mark 5. Grease a 2-litre/3½-pint baking dish with butter.

For the cheese sauce, melt the butter in a saucepan over a medium heat and add the flour. Cook, stirring, for about 3 minutes. Slowly whisk in the cold milk. Continue whisking until there are no visible lumps. Add the nutmeg, cayenne pepper and thyme. The sauce will thicken as it comes back to a simmer. Reduce the heat to low and simmer, stirring occasionally, for 10 minutes.

Turn off the heat and stir in the cheese. When all the cheese has melted into the sauce, add the salt and set aside until needed.

Bring a large saucepan of water to a rapid boil. Add the broccoli and cook for about 5 minutes or just until the stalk ends begin to get tender. Do not overcook, as the broccoli will cook further in the oven. Drain very well (otherwise the bake will be watery). Transfer to a large mixing bowl.

Pour over the cheese sauce and fold with a palette knife until the broccoli is completely coated with the sauce. Transfer to the prepared baking dish. Combine the breadcrumbs, melted butter and Parmesan in a small bowl. Sprinkle evenly over the top and bake in the preheated oven for 25 minutes or until the top is browned and bubbly.

Potato & Egg Salad

serves 10

1.8 kg/4 lb new potatoes, scrubbed and halved

3 hard-boiled eggs, chopped

115 g/4 oz celery, diced

25 g/1 oz spring onions, white and light green parts only, finely chopped

275 g/9¾ oz mayonnaise

2 tbsp cider vinegar

1 tbsp Dijon mustard

1½ tsp salt

½ tsp sugar

¼ tsp black pepper

Pinch of cayenne pepper (optional)

Boil the potatoes in a large saucepan of water until just tender, then drain well and leave to cool to room temperature. Cut into 2.5-cm/1-inch pieces and place in a large bowl. Add the eggs and celery.

Combine the rest of the ingredients in a small mixing bowl. Pour over the potato mixture and use a palette knife to thoroughly combine.

Chill in the refrigerator for at least 1 hour before serving.

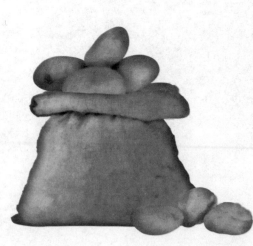

Roast Vegetables

serves 6-8

4 tbsp olive oil

1 garlic clove, peeled, left whole but crushed slightly

2 large red peppers, deseeded and cut into 1-cm/½-inch strips

4 courgettes, halved, then cut lengthways into quarters

1 red onion, peeled and cut into eighths

900 g/2 lb Desiree, King Edward or Maris Piper potatoes, cut into wedges

4 carrots, peeled, cut into thirds, then into 1-cm/½-inch sticks

Juice of ½ lemon

1 tsp chopped fresh rosemary

2 tbsp chopped fresh parsley, plus extra to garnish

Salt and pepper

Preheat the oven to 230°C/450°F/Gas Mark 8. Line 1–2 baking trays with foil.

In a small saucepan, warm the oil and garlic over a low heat. Turn off the heat and leave to infuse for 30 minutes. Remove and discard the garlic clove and reserve the oil.

Put the remaining ingredients into a large mixing bowl, along with the garlic oil. Toss to coat completely.

Arrange the vegetables in a single layer on the prepared baking trays. Roast in the preheated oven for 20 minutes. Remove and stir the vegetables so they cook evenly. Return to the oven and roast for a further 25–35 minutes or until the vegetables are tender and the edges are browned.

Season to taste with salt and pepper. Serve hot, sprinkled with chopped parsley.

Pepper & Sweetcorn Salad

serves 6-8

3 tbsp olive oil

450 g/1 lb fresh sweetcorn kernels

400 g/14 oz canned black beans, drained and rinsed

1 red pepper, deseeded and finely diced

1 orange pepper, deseeded and finely diced

1 fresh jalapeño chilli, deseeded and finely chopped

4 spring onions, thinly sliced

1 garlic clove, crushed

2 tbsp chopped fresh coriander

½ tsp ground cumin

¼ tsp chipotle pepper, or to taste

3 tbsp lime juice

1 tbsp rice vinegar

1 tsp sugar

1 tsp salt, or to taste

Heat the oil in a large, non-stick saucepan over a medium–high heat. Add the sweetcorn and sauté, stirring, for about 3–4 minutes.

Remove the pan from the heat and transfer the sweetcorn to a large mixing bowl. Add the rest of the ingredients and toss to combine thoroughly.

Refrigerate for at least 4 hours. Just before serving, toss well, then taste and adjust the seasoning, adding extra chipotle and salt if needed.

Cornbread

serves 6

115 g/4 oz unsalted butter, melted, plus extra for greasing

125 g/4½ oz granulated sugar

2 eggs

225 ml/8 fl oz buttermilk

½ tsp bicarbonate of soda

125 g/4½ oz plain flour

150 g/5½ oz polenta

½ tsp salt

Preheat the oven to 190°C/375°F/Gas Mark 5. Grease a 25-cm/10-inch cast-iron frying pan with butter.

In a large mixing bowl, whisk together the melted butter and sugar. Add the eggs and whisk until combined. Add the buttermilk and bicarbonate of soda and whisk to combine. Add the flour, polenta and salt. Using a palette knife, stir until just blended. Do not over mix.

Pour the mixture into the prepared frying pan and bake in the preheated oven for about 35 minutes or until a skewer inserted in the centre comes out clean.

Leave to cool for at least 15 minutes before cutting into thick wedges.

Warm Bacon & Egg Salad

serves 4

2 hearts of cos lettuce,
roughly torn

4 eggs

2 tbsp sunflower oil

2 thick slices of bread,
crusts removed and
cubed

200 g/7 oz smoked
bacon, cubed

12 cherry tomatoes,
halved

For the dressing

2 tbsp extra virgin olive
oil

1 tbsp red wine vinegar

1 tsp Dijon mustard

Pepper

For the dressing, put all the ingredients into a small
screw-top jar and shake until well blended. Put the lettuce
leaves in a salad bowl.

Place the eggs in a saucepan and cover with cold water.
Bring to the boil and boil for 4 minutes. Drain and plunge
the eggs into cold water for 2 minutes. Peel off the shells
and cut into quarters.

Heat the sunflower oil in a large frying pan and fry the
bread cubes for 3–4 minutes, turning frequently, until
golden brown. Remove the croûtons with a slotted spoon
and set aside.

Add the bacon cubes to the pan and fry over a medium–
high heat until crisp and golden. Add the tomatoes and
dressing to the pan and cook for a further minute.

Gently toss the bacon, tomatoes and dressing with the
lettuce leaves. Add the quartered eggs and scatter over the
croûtons. Serve immediately.

Buttermilk Scones

makes 12-14

250 g/9 oz plain flour, plus extra for dusting

2 tsp baking powder

¼ tsp bicarbonate of soda

1 tsp salt

100 g/3½ oz unsalted butter, cut into thin slices, chilled in freezer

175 ml/6 fl oz cold buttermilk, plus extra for brushing

Preheat the oven to 220°C/425°F/Gas Mark 7. Line a baking tray with baking paper.

In a mixing bowl, mix together the dry ingredients to thoroughly combine. Cut in the butter slices, using a pair of knives, until the mixture resembles coarse breadcrumbs.

Make a well in the centre and pour in the buttermilk. Stir the dry ingredients into the buttermilk with a fork until a loose, sticky dough is formed. Stop as soon as the mixture comes together. Form into a ball and turn the dough out onto a floured work surface.

With floured hands, pat the dough into a rectangle measuring about 20 x 10 cm/8 x 4 inches. Fold the dough into thirds. Repeat this process twice more.

On a lightly floured work surface, roll or pat the dough out until it is about 1 cm/½ inch thick. Cut into rounds, using a biscuit cutter, and place on the prepared baking tray, spaced well apart. Gather up any dough trimmings to make a few more scones.

Make a slight depression in the centre of each scone with your thumb to help them rise evenly. Lightly brush the tops with buttermilk. Bake in the preheated oven for about 15 minutes or until risen and golden brown. Transfer to a wire rack and leave to cool for 10 minutes before serving.

Roast Red Potato Salad

serves 6

1 kg/2 lb 4 oz small red potatoes, scrubbed

1 tbsp chopped fresh flat-leaf parsley

1 tbsp chopped fresh tarragon

1 tbsp snipped fresh chives

1 tsp very finely chopped fresh thyme leaves

Salt and pepper

For the dressing

2 garlic cloves, very finely chopped

1 tsp Dijon mustard

Pinch of cayenne pepper

4 tbsp white wine vinegar

150 ml/5 fl oz olive oil

Preheat the oven to 200°C/400°F/Gas Mark 6.

Place the potatoes in a roasting tin. Bake in the preheated oven for 25–30 minutes or until tender (time will vary depending on size).

Meanwhile, make the dressing. Place the garlic, mustard, cayenne pepper and vinegar in a large mixing bowl. Whisk in the oil, very slowly at first, in a steady stream until incorporated.

When the potatoes are just cool enough to handle, cut into halves or quarters. Add the potatoes to the bowl and toss in the dressing, along with salt and pepper to taste. Leave to stand for 15 minutes. Add the herbs and toss again.

Cover and refrigerate for at least 2 hours or overnight. Just before serving, toss well, then taste and adjust the seasoning, adding extra salt and pepper if needed.

Country Loaf

7-g/¼-oz sachet easy-blend dried yeast

¼ tsp sugar

300 ml/10 fl oz warm water

300–375 g/10–13 oz strong white flour, plus extra for dusting

1 tsp salt

1 tsp vegetable oil

Polenta, for sprinkling

Place the yeast, sugar, warm water and 175 g/6 oz of the flour in a large mixing bowl. Stir together until smooth, cover with a clean tea towel and leave in a warm place for 2 hours.

Add 125 g/4½ oz of the remaining flour and the salt to the bowl and stir to form a sticky dough. Turn the dough out onto a well-floured work surface. Knead the dough for about 10 minutes, adding the remaining 75 g/2¾ oz flour, but only as needed to stop the dough sticking to the surface or your hands. You want a very soft, elastic dough, so use the flour very sparingly.

Grease a large bowl with the oil. Shape the dough into a ball and place into the bowl, turning over a few times so the dough is lightly oiled. Cover the bowl with a tea towel and leave to rise in a warm place for about 2 hours until it doubles in size.

Generously sprinkle a baking tray with polenta. Punch down the dough and turn out onto a lightly floured work surface. Shape into an oval and place on the prepared baking tray, seam-side down. Dust the top of the loaf lightly with flour and cover with a tea towel. Allow to rise for 1 hour in a warm place. Meanwhile, preheat the oven to 220°C/425°F/Gas Mark 7.

Place a cake tin half-filled with water on the bottom rack of the oven. Bake the bread in the centre of the preheated oven for 45 minutes or until browned. Turn out onto a wire rack and leave to cool completely before slicing.

Glazed Yams

serves 6-8

Juice of 1 lemon

1 kg/2 lb 4 oz orange-fleshed yams

25 g/1 oz unsalted butter, plus extra for greasing

4 tbsp muscovado sugar

½ tsp salt, or to taste

Pinch of cayenne pepper

Preheat the oven to 180°C/350°F/Gas Mark 4. Lightly grease a baking dish.

Place the lemon juice in a large bowl. Peel the yams, cut into 2.5-cm/1-inch cubes and toss with the lemon juice.

Melt the butter in a large frying pan over a medium–high heat. Add the yams, lemon juice, sugar, salt and cayenne pepper. Cook, stirring, for about 5–7 minutes, until a sticky syrup is formed and the edges of the yams begin to caramelize.

Remove from the heat and transfer to the prepared baking dish. Bake in the preheated oven for 20–25 minutes or until tender. Serve hot.

Garlic & Herb Potato Wedges

serves 4

4 Desiree, King Edward or Maris Piper potatoes, scrubbed

3 tbsp olive oil

4 garlic cloves, crushed

½ tsp dried rosemary, finely crushed

½ tsp dried oregano

½ tsp dried thyme

½ tsp paprika

½ tsp pepper

1 tsp salt, or to taste

Preheat the oven to 220°C/425°F/Gas Mark 7. Line a large roasting tin with foil.

Cut each potato in half lengthways. Cut each half into 4 equal-sized wedges. Place the potato wedges in a large mixing bowl with the rest of the ingredients. Toss well to coat the potatoes evenly.

Place the potato wedges, skin-side down, in the prepared tin, spacing them well apart so they cook evenly.

Bake in the preheated oven for 35–40 minutes or until well browned, crispy and tender. Serve immediately, sprinkled with more salt if wished.

Something Sweet

Cinnamon Swirl & Soured Cream Bundt Cake

serves 6-8

280 g/10 oz plain flour, plus extra for dusting

1 tsp baking powder

1 tsp bicarbonate of soda

½ tsp salt

175 g/6 oz unsalted butter, plus extra for greasing

300 g/10½ oz caster sugar

3 eggs

225 g/8 oz soured cream

1 tsp vanilla extract

55 g/2 oz chopped walnuts (optional)

For the swirl

1 tbsp ground cinnamon

3 tbsp soft light brown sugar

2 tbsp granulated sugar

For the glaze

115 g/4 oz icing sugar

About 1½ tbsp milk

1 tsp ground cinnamon, or to taste

Preheat the oven to 180°C/350°F/Gas Mark 4. Grease a 25-cm/10-inch bundt tin and lightly dust with flour.

Sift together the flour, baking powder, bicarbonate of soda and salt into a large bowl, then set aside until needed.

Cream the butter and sugar together until light and fluffy. Beat in the eggs, one at a time, mixing thoroughly before adding the next. Beat in the soured cream and vanilla extract until combined. Add the flour mixture, stirring until just combined. Stir in the walnuts, if using.

Pour half the mixture into the prepared tin and spread evenly. Mix the ingredients for the swirl in a small bowl. Sprinkle evenly around the centre of the mixture in the tin. Cover with the remaining cake mixture.

Bake in the preheated oven for 50 minutes or until a skewer inserted in the centre comes out clean. Leave to cool for 20 minutes before removing from the tin.

For the glaze, put the icing sugar into a small mixing bowl and stir in enough milk to create a thick but pourable glaze. Stir in the cinnamon. Drizzle over the top of the cake. Once the glaze is set, slice and serve with a hot drink.

Double Fudge Brownies

150 g/5½ oz plain chocolate (at least 70% cocoa solids), broken into small pieces

75 g/2¾ oz unsalted butter, cut into pieces, plus extra for greasing

200 g/7 oz caster sugar

¼ tsp salt

2 tbsp water

2 eggs

1 tsp vanilla extract

100 g/3½ oz plain flour

55 g/2 oz walnuts, chopped (optional)

Preheat the oven to 160°C/325°F/Gas Mark 3. Grease a 20-cm/8-inch square baking dish.

Place the chocolate, butter, sugar, salt and water in a small saucepan over a very low heat. Heat, stirring often, until the chocolate and butter are melted.

Pour the chocolate mixture into a mixing bowl. Stir in the eggs, one at a time, then add the vanilla extract. Stir in the flour, followed by the walnuts, if using.

Pour the mixture into the prepared baking dish. Bake in the preheated oven for 35 minutes. Leave to cool completely before cutting into squares.

Peach Cobbler

For the filling
6 peaches, peeled and sliced

4 tbsp granulated sugar

½ tbsp lemon juice

1½ tsp cornflour

½ tsp almond or vanilla extract

Ice cream, to serve

For the topping
200 g/7 oz plain flour

100 g/3½ oz granulated sugar

1½ tsp baking powder

½ tsp salt

85 g/3 oz unsalted butter, diced

1 egg

5–6 tbsp milk

Preheat the oven to 220°C/425°F/Gas Mark 7.

Place the peaches in a 23-cm/9-inch square baking dish. Add the sugar, lemon juice, cornflour and almond extract and toss together. Bake in the preheated oven for 20 minutes.

Meanwhile, to make the topping, sift the flour, all but 2 tablespoons of the sugar, the baking powder and the salt into a bowl. Rub in the butter with your fingertips until the mixture resembles breadcrumbs. Mix the egg and 5 tablespoons of the milk in a jug, then mix into the dry ingredients with a fork until a soft, sticky dough forms. If the dough seems too dry, stir in the extra tablespoon of milk.

Reduce the oven temperature to 200°C/400°F/Gas Mark 6. Remove the peaches from the oven and drop spoonfuls of the topping over the surface, without smoothing. Sprinkle with the remaining sugar, return to the oven and bake for a further 15 minutes or until the topping is golden brown and firm — the topping will spread as it cooks. Serve hot or at room temperature with ice cream.

Magic Lemon Sponge Cake

serves 4

140 g/5 oz caster sugar

3 eggs, separated

300 ml/10 fl oz milk

3 tbsp self-raising flour, sifted

150 ml/5 fl oz lemon juice

Icing sugar, for dusting

Using an electric mixer, beat the sugar with the egg yolks in a bowl. Gradually beat in the milk, followed by the flour and lemon juice.

Whisk the egg whites in a separate grease-free bowl until stiff. Fold half the whites into the yolk mixture, using a palette knife in a figure-of-eight movement, then fold in the remainder. Try not to knock out the air.

Pour the mixture into a heatproof bowl and cover with foil. Stand the bowl on a trivet in the slow cooker and pour in enough boiling water to come about one third of the way up the side of the bowl. Cover and cook on high for 2½ hours, until the mixture has set and the sauce and sponge have separated.

Carefully remove the bowl from the slow cooker and discard the foil. Transfer to warmed bowls, lightly dust with icing sugar and serve immediately.

New York Cheesecake with Fruit Sauce

serves 8-10

115 g/4 oz unsalted butter, plus extra for greasing

200 g/7 oz digestive biscuits, finely crushed

250 g/9 oz plus 1 tbsp caster sugar

900 g/2 lb cream cheese

2 tbsp plain flour

1 tsp vanilla extract

Finely grated rind of 1 orange

Finely grated rind of 1 lemon

3 eggs

2 egg yolks

300 ml/10 fl oz double cream

For the sauce

115 g/4 oz berries, such as blackberries or raspberries

2 tbsp water

2 tbsp caster sugar

2 tbsp fruit liqueur, such as crème de cassis or crème de framboise

Preheat the oven to 180°C/350°F/Gas Mark 4. Grease a 23-cm/9-inch round cake tin.

Melt the butter in a saucepan over a low heat. Remove from the heat and stir in the crushed biscuits and the 1 tablespoon of sugar. Press the biscuit mixture into the base of the prepared cake tin. Bake in the preheated oven for 10 minutes. Remove from the oven and leave to cool.

Increase the oven temperature to 200°C/400°F/Gas Mark 6. With an electric mixer, beat the cream cheese until soft, then gradually add the sugar and flour and beat until smooth. Add the vanilla extract, orange rind and lemon rind, then beat in the eggs and egg yolks, 1 at a time. Finally beat in the cream. The mixture should be light and fluffy.

Pour the filling into the tin, on top of the biscuit base. Transfer to the oven and bake for 15 minutes. Reduce the heat to 110°C/225°F/Gas Mark ¼ and bake for a further 30 minutes. Turn the oven off and leave the cheesecake to cool in the oven for 2 hours. Cover and chill overnight.

For the sauce, put all the ingredients in a small, heavy-based pan and heat gently until the sugar has dissolved and the fruit juices run. Process to a paste in a food processor, then push through a non-metallic sieve to remove the seeds. Serve warm or cold with the cheesecake.

Boston Cream Pie

225 g/8 oz self-raising
flour

½ tsp salt

1 tsp baking powder

115 g/4 oz unsalted
butter, softened, plus
extra for greasing

200 g/7 oz caster sugar

2 eggs, beaten

175 ml/6 fl oz milk

For the pastry cream

100 g/3½ oz caster
sugar

2 tbsp cornflour

3 eggs

225 ml/8 fl oz double
cream

225 ml/8 fl oz milk

15 g/½ oz unsalted
butter

1½ tsp vanilla extract

Pinch of salt

For the chocolate
topping

115 g/4 oz plain
chocolate, broken into
pieces

125 ml/4 fl oz double
cream

1 tsp unsalted butter

For the pastry cream, whisk together the sugar, cornflour and eggs until the whisk leaves a ribbon trail when lifted. Set aside. Bring the cream, milk and butter to the boil in a pan. Add the sugar mixture and boil, whisking constantly, for 1 minute until thickened, then strain into a bowl. Cover the surface with clingfilm and chill overnight.

Preheat the oven to 190°C/375°F/Gas Mark 5. Grease 2 x 20-cm/8-inch sandwich tins. Sift the flour, salt and baking powder into a bowl and set aside.

Cream together the butter and sugar in a separate bowl until pale and fluffy. Gradually add the eggs, mixing well after each addition. Gradually add the milk, alternating with the flour mixture, and stir to combine. Divide the mixture between the prepared tins. Bake in the preheated oven for 25 minutes until well risen and firm to the touch. Turn out onto a wire rack and leave to cool.

Put the chocolate into a heatproof bowl. Bring the cream and butter to simmering point in a small saucepan, then pour over the chocolate. Leave to stand for 3 minutes, then whisk gently to mix. Leave to cool and thicken. Whisk the vanilla extract and salt into the pastry cream, then spread it over 1 of the cakes. Top with the second cake, then spread with the chocolate topping.

Crème Brûlée

1 vanilla pod

1 litre/1¾ pints double cream

6 egg yolks

100 g/3½ oz caster sugar

85 g/3 oz soft light brown sugar

Using a sharp knife, split the vanilla pod in half lengthways, scrape the seeds into a saucepan and add the pod. Pour in the cream and bring just to the boil, stirring constantly. Remove from the heat, cover and leave to infuse for 20 minutes.

Whisk together the egg yolks and caster sugar in a bowl until thoroughly mixed. Remove and discard the vanilla pod from the pan, then whisk the cream into the egg yolk mixture. Strain the mixture into a large jug.

Divide the mixture between 6 ramekins and cover with foil. Stand the ramekins on a trivet in the slow cooker and pour in enough boiling water to come about halfway up the sides of the ramekins. Cover and cook on low for 3–3½ hours until just set. Remove the slow cooker pot from the base unit and leave to cool completely, then remove the ramekins and chill in the refrigerator for at least 4 hours.

Preheat the grill. Sprinkle the brown sugar evenly over the surface of each pudding, then cook under the preheated grill for 30–60 seconds until the sugar has melted and caramelized. Alternatively, you can use a cook's blowtorch. Return the dishes to the refrigerator and chill for a further hour before serving.

Almond Sponge Cake

Unsalted butter, for greasing

10–12 sponge fingers

300 ml/10 fl oz milk

2 eggs

2 tbsp caster sugar

55 g/2 oz blanched almonds, chopped

4–5 drops of almond extract

For the sherry sauce

1 tbsp caster sugar

3 egg yolks

150 ml/5 fl oz sweet sherry

Grease a 600-ml/1-pint pudding basin. Line the basin with the sponge fingers, cutting them to fit and placing them cut-side down and sugar-coated sides outwards. Cover the base of the basin with some of the trimmings.

Pour the milk into a saucepan and bring just to the boil, then remove from the heat. Beat together the eggs and sugar in a heatproof bowl until combined, then stir in the milk. Stir in the almonds and almond extract.

Carefully pour the mixture into the prepared basin, making sure that the sponge fingers stay in place, and cover the basin with foil. Place the basin on a trivet in the slow cooker and pour in enough boiling water to come about halfway up the side of the dish. Cover and cook on high for 3–3½ hours until set.

Shortly before serving, make the sherry sauce. Put the sugar, egg yolks and sherry into a heatproof bowl. Set the basin over a saucepan of simmering water, without letting the base of the bowl touch the surface of the water. Whisk well until the mixture thickens, but do not let it boil. Remove from the heat.

Carefully remove the basin from the slow cooker and discard the foil. Leave to stand for 2–3 minutes, then turn out onto a warmed serving plate. Pour the sherry sauce around it and serve immediately.

Blackberry & Apple Loaf Cake

serves 8-10

**Unsalted butter,
for greasing**

**350 g/12 oz cooking
apples**

3 tbsp lemon juice

**250 g/9 oz plain
wholemeal flour**

2½ tsp baking powder

**1 tsp ground cinnamon,
plus extra for dusting**

**140 g/5 oz blackberries,
thawed if frozen**

**225 g/8 oz soft light
brown sugar**

1 egg, lightly beaten

**175 g/6 oz low-fat
natural yogurt**

**55 g/2 oz demerara
sugar**

Preheat the oven to 190°C/375°F/Gas Mark 5. Grease a
23 x 13 x 10-cm/9 x 5 x 4-inch loaf tin and line with
baking paper.

Core, peel and finely dice the apples. Place them in a
saucepan with the lemon juice and bring to the boil. Cover
and simmer for 10 minutes until soft. Beat well to form a
smooth purée. Set aside to cool.

Sift the flour, baking powder and cinnamon into a
bowl, adding any bran that remains in the sieve. Stir in
100 g/3½ oz of the blackberries and the brown sugar.
Make a well in the centre of the ingredients and add the
egg, yogurt and cooled apple purée. Mix until thoroughly
blended. Spoon the mixture into the prepared loaf tin and
smooth over the top with a palette knife.

Sprinkle with the remaining blackberries, pressing them
down into the cake mixture, and top the mixture with the
demerara sugar.

Bake in the preheated oven for 40–45 minutes until a
skewer inserted in the centre comes out clean. Leave to
cool in the tin.

Turn the cake out of the tin. Serve dusted with cinnamon.

Chocolate Pots

serves 6

300 ml/10 fl oz single cream

300 ml/10 fl oz milk

225 g/8 oz plain chocolate (at least 70% cocoa solids), broken into small pieces

1 large egg

4 egg yolks

55 g/2 oz caster sugar

150 ml/5 fl oz double cream

Chocolate curls, to decorate

Pour the single cream and milk into a saucepan and add the chocolate. Set the pan over a very low heat and stir until the chocolate has melted and the mixture is smooth. Remove from the heat and leave to cool for 10 minutes.

Beat together the egg, egg yolks and sugar in a bowl until combined. Gradually stir in the chocolate mixture until thoroughly blended. Strain into a jug.

Divide the mixture between 6 ramekins and cover with foil. Stand the ramekins on a trivet in the slow cooker and pour in enough boiling water to come about halfway up the sides of the ramekins. Cover and cook on low for 3–3½ hours until just set. Remove the slow cooker pot from the base unit and leave to cool completely, then remove the ramekins and chill in the refrigerator for at least 4 hours.

Whip the double cream until it holds soft peaks. Top each chocolate pot with a little of the cream and decorate with chocolate curls. Serve immediately.

Poached Peaches in Marsala Wine

serves 4-6

150 ml/5 fl oz plus 2 tbsp water

150 ml/5 fl oz Marsala wine

55 g/2 oz caster sugar

1 vanilla pod, split lengthways

6 peaches, cut into wedges

2 tsp cornflour

Greek-style yogurt, to serve

Pour the 150 ml/5 fl oz of water and the Marsala wine into a saucepan and add the sugar and vanilla pod. Set the pan over a low heat and stir until the sugar has dissolved, then bring to the boil without stirring. Remove from the heat.

Put the peaches into the slow cooker and pour the syrup over them. Cover and cook on high for 1–1½ hours until the fruit is tender.

Using a slotted spoon, gently transfer the peaches to a serving dish. Remove the vanilla pod from the slow cooker and scrape the seeds into the syrup with the point of a knife. Discard the pod. Stir the cornflour to a paste with the 2 tablespoons of water in a small bowl, then stir into the syrup. Re-cover and cook on high for 15 minutes, stirring occasionally.

Spoon the syrup over the fruit and leave to cool. Serve warm or chill in the refrigerator for 2 hours before serving with yogurt.

Apple Crumble

serves 4

55 g/2 oz plain flour

55 g/2 oz rolled oats

150 g/5½ oz soft light
brown sugar

½ tsp freshly grated
nutmeg

½ tsp ground cinnamon

115 g/4 oz unsalted
butter, softened

4 cooking apples,
peeled, cored and sliced

4–5 tbsp apple juice

Greek-style yogurt,
to serve

Sift the flour into a bowl and stir in the oats, sugar, nutmeg and cinnamon. Add the butter and mix in with a fork.

Place the apple slices in the bottom of the slow cooker and add the apple juice. Sprinkle the crumble mixture evenly over them.

Cover and cook on low for 5½ hours. Serve hot, warm or cold with yogurt.

Madeira Cake with Orange Glaze

serves 6

250 g/9 oz plain flour, plus extra for dusting

1 tsp baking powder

¼ tsp bicarbonate of soda

½ tsp salt

225 g/8 oz unsalted butter, plus extra for greasing

250 g/9 oz caster sugar

1 tbsp grated lemon rind

1 tbsp grated orange rind

4 eggs

125 ml/4 fl oz buttermilk

For the glaze

125 g/4½ oz icing sugar

About 1½ tbsp orange juice

1 tbsp grated orange rind

Preheat the oven to 160°C/325°F/Gas Mark 3. Grease a 23 x 13 x 10-cm/9 x 5 x 4-inch loaf tin and dust with flour.

Sift together the flour, baking powder, bicarbonate of soda and salt into a bowl. Set aside.

In a separate large bowl, use an electric mixer to beat the butter, sugar, lemon rind and orange rind until very light and creamy. Beat in the eggs, one at a time, beating very thoroughly after each addition. Use a palette knife to stir in the flour mixture alternately with the buttermilk, ending with flour. Spoon the mixture into the prepared loaf tin.

Bake in the preheated oven for 1 hour–1 hour 15 minutes or until a skewer inserted in the centre comes out clean. Remove and leave to rest for 15 minutes, then turn out onto a wire rack. Leave to cool a further 15 minutes before glazing.

Stir together the glaze ingredients, adding enough of the orange juice to get a smooth, spreadable consistency. Apply to the top of the warm cake. Leave the cake to cool completely before slicing.

Sweet Potato Pie

serves 8-10

For the pastry

175 g/6 oz plain flour, plus extra for dusting

½ tsp salt

¼ tsp caster sugar

50 g/1¾ oz cold unsalted butter, diced

40 g/1½ oz cold white vegetable fat, diced

2–2½ tbsp ice-cold water

For the filling

500 g/1 lb 2 oz orange-fleshed sweet potatoes, scrubbed

3 large eggs, beaten

100 g/3½ oz soft light brown sugar

350 ml/12 fl oz canned evaporated milk

40 g/1½ oz unsalted butter, melted

2 tsp vanilla extract

1 tsp ground cinnamon

1 tsp freshly grated nutmeg

½ tsp salt

Freshly whipped cream, to serve

To make the pastry, sift the flour, salt and sugar into a bowl. Add the butter and vegetable fat to the bowl and rub in with your fingertips until the mixture resembles fine breadcrumbs. Sprinkle over 2 tablespoons of the water and mix with a fork until a soft dough forms. Add the remaining water if the dough is too dry. Wrap in clingfilm and chill for at least 1 hour.

Meanwhile, bring a large saucepan of water to the boil over a high heat. Add the sweet potatoes and cook for 15 minutes. Drain, then cool them under cold running water. When cool, peel and then mash. Beat in the eggs and sugar until very smooth. Beat in the remaining ingredients, except the whipped cream, then set aside until required.

Preheat the oven to 220°C/425°F/Gas Mark 7. Roll out the pastry on a lightly floured work surface into a thin round and use to line a 23-cm/9-inch pie dish, about 4 cm/1½ inches high. Trim off the excess pastry and press a fork around the edge. Prick the base of the pastry case all over with the fork. Line with baking paper, fill with baking beans and bake in the preheated oven for 12 minutes or until lightly golden. Remove the pastry case from the oven and take out the beans and paper. Pour the filling into the pastry case and return to the oven for 10 minutes. Reduce the temperature to 160°C/325°F/Gas Mark 3 and bake for a further 35 minutes or until a knife inserted into the centre comes out clean.

Leave to cool on a wire rack. Serve warm or at room temperature with whipped cream.

Lemon Meringue Pie

serves 8-10

Unsalted butter, for greasing

250 g/9 oz ready-made shortcrust pastry, thawed if frozen

Plain flour, for dusting

3 tbsp cornflour

100 g/3½ oz caster sugar

Grated rind of 3 lemons

300 ml/10 fl oz water

150 ml/5 fl oz lemon juice

3 egg yolks

55 g/2 oz unsalted butter, diced

For the meringue

3 egg whites

200 g/7 oz caster sugar

1 tsp soft light brown sugar

Preheat the oven to 200°C/400°F/Gas Mark 6.

Grease a 25-cm/10-inch fluted tart tin. Roll out the pastry on a lightly floured work surface into a round 5 cm/ 2 inches larger than the tin. Ease the pastry into the tin, press down lightly into the corners and trim the edge. Prick the base with a fork and chill, uncovered, in the refrigerator for 20–30 minutes. Line the pastry case with baking paper, fill with baking beans and bake in the preheated oven for 15 minutes. Remove the beans and paper and return the pastry case to the oven for 10 minutes or until the pastry is dry and just coloured. Remove from the oven and reduce the temperature to 150°C/300°F/Gas Mark 2.

Put the cornflour, sugar and lemon rind in a saucepan. Pour in a little of the water and blend to a smooth paste. Gradually add the remaining water and the lemon juice. Bring the mixture to the boil over a medium heat, stirring constantly. Simmer gently for 1 minute or until smooth and glossy. Remove from the heat and beat in the egg yolks, one at a time, then beat in the butter. Put the pan in a bowl of cold water to cool the filling. When cool, spoon into the pastry case.

For the meringue, whisk the egg whites with an electric mixer until soft peaks form. Add the caster sugar gradually, whisking well with each addition, until glossy and firm. Spoon over the filling to cover it completely. Swirl the meringue into peaks and sprinkle with the brown sugar. Bake for 20–30 minutes or until the meringue is crispy and pale gold but still soft in the centre.

Chocolate & Walnut Sponge Cake

serves 4-6

55 g/2 oz cocoa powder, plus extra for dusting

2 tbsp milk

115 g/4 oz self-raising flour

Pinch of salt

115 g/4 oz unsalted butter, softened, plus extra for greasing

115 g/4 oz caster sugar

2 eggs, lightly beaten

55 g/2 oz chopped walnuts

Whipped cream, to serve

Grease a 1.2-litre/2-pint pudding basin. Cut out a double round of greaseproof paper that is 7.5 cm/3 inches wider than the rim of the basin. Grease one side and make a pleat in the centre.

Mix the cocoa with the milk to a paste in a small bowl. Sift the flour and salt into a separate small bowl.

Beat together the butter and sugar in a large bowl until pale and fluffy. Gradually beat in the eggs, a little at a time, then gently fold in the sifted flour mixture, followed by the cocoa mixture and the walnuts.

Spoon the mixture into the prepared basin. Cover the basin with the greaseproof paper round, greased-side down, and tie in place with kitchen string. Stand the basin on a trivet in the slow cooker and pour in enough boiling water to come about halfway up the side of the basin. Cover and cook on high for 3–3½ hours.

Carefully remove the basin from the slow cooker and discard the greaseproof paper. Run a knife around the inside of the basin, then turn out onto a warmed serving dish. Serve immediately with whipped cream, dusted with cocoa.

Crêpes with Apples

serves 4

125 g/4½ oz plain flour
Pinch of salt
1 tsp finely grated lemon rind
1 egg
300 ml/10 fl oz milk
1–2 tbsp vegetable oil, plus extra for brushing

For the filling
1 cooking apple, peeled, cored and sliced
2 tbsp raisins

For the sauce
55 g/2 oz unsalted butter
3 tbsp golden syrup
70 g/2½ oz light muscovado sugar
1 tbsp rum or brandy (optional)
1 tbsp lemon juice

Preheat the oven to 160°C/325°F/Gas Mark 3. Brush a baking dish with a little oil.

Sift the flour and salt into a bowl. Add the lemon rind, egg and milk and whisk to make a smooth batter.

Heat a little of the oil in a heavy-based frying pan. Pour in just enough of the batter to cover the base of the pan in a thin, even layer. Cook until the underside is golden, then flip and cook on the other side until golden brown. Repeat until all the batter has been used (it should make 8 thin crêpes). Stack the crêpes, interleaved with kitchen paper, and keep warm.

To make the filling, cook the apples and raisins in a little water over a low heat until soft. Divide the mixture evenly between the crêpes and roll up or fold into triangles. Arrange in the prepared dish. Bake in the preheated oven for about 15 minutes until warmed through.

To make the sauce, melt the butter, golden syrup and sugar together in a saucepan, stirring well. Add the rum, if using, and lemon juice. Do not allow the mixture to boil. Serve the crêpes on warmed plates with a little sauce poured over.

Butterscotch Blondies

makes 9

125 g/4½ oz plain flour

Pinch of bicarbonate of soda

½ tsp baking powder

¼ tsp salt

115 g/4 oz unsalted butter, melted, plus extra for greasing

175 g/6 oz soft light brown sugar

55 g/2 oz caster sugar

1 egg plus 1 egg yolk, beaten together

1 tsp vanilla extract

85 g/3 oz butterscotch chips

40 g/1½ oz milk chocolate chips

30 g/1 oz dry-roasted cashews, chopped

Preheat the oven to 180°C/350°F/Gas Mark 4. Lightly grease a 20-cm/8-inch square baking tin or dish.

Sift the flour, bicarbonate of soda, baking powder and salt into a large bowl. Set aside.

In a separate large bowl, whisk together the melted butter and sugars until combined. Add the egg, egg yolk and vanilla extract and stir to combine. Using a wooden spoon, stir in the flour mixture. Fold in the butterscotch chips, chocolate chips and cashews.

With a palette knife, scrape the mixture into the prepared tin. Smooth to distribute evenly. Bake in the preheated oven for about 35 minutes or until the top is golden brown and a skewer inserted in the centre comes out clean.

Leave to cool completely before cutting into bars.

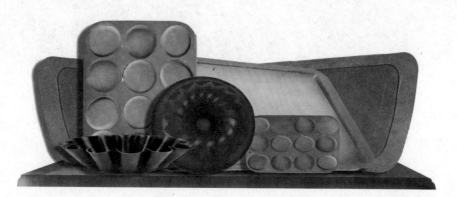

Blushing Pears

6 small ripe pears

225 ml/8 fl oz ruby port

200 g/7 oz caster sugar

1 tsp finely chopped crystallized ginger

2 tbsp lemon juice

Whipped cream, to serve

Peel the pears, cut them in half lengthways and scoop out the cores. Place them in the slow cooker.

Combine the port, sugar, ginger and lemon juice in a jug and pour the mixture over the pears. Cover and cook on low for 4 hours until the pears are tender.

Leave the pears to cool in the slow cooker, then carefully transfer to a bowl and chill in the refrigerator until required.

To serve, cut each pear half into about 6 slices lengthways, leaving the fruit intact at the stalk end. Carefully lift the pear halves onto serving plates and press gently to fan out the slices. Spoon the cooking juices over the pears and serve immediately with cream.

Rice Pudding

serves 4

140 g/5 oz pudding rice

1 litre/1¾ pints milk

115 g/4 oz granulated sugar

1 tsp vanilla extract

Ground cinnamon, to decorate

Rinse the rice well under cold running water and drain thoroughly. Pour the milk into a large, heavy-based saucepan, add the sugar and bring to the boil, stirring constantly. Sprinkle in the rice, stir well and simmer gently for 10–15 minutes. Transfer the mixture to a heatproof bowl and cover with foil.

Stand the bowl on a trivet in the slow cooker and pour in enough boiling water to come about one third of the way up the side of the bowl. Cover and cook on high for 2 hours.

Carefully remove the bowl from the slow cooker and discard the foil. Stir the vanilla extract into the rice, then spoon it into warmed bowls. Lightly dust with cinnamon and serve immediately.

Index

almonds
  Almond Sponge Cake 196
  Pork with Almonds 125
apples
  Apple Crumble 202
  Blackberry & Apple Loaf Cake 197
  Braised Red Cabbage & Apples 145
  Chicken Braised with Red Cabbage 110
  Crêpes with Apples 210
  Pork with Apple & Herbs 87
  Waldorf Salad 154
apricots
  Pork with Peppers & Apricots 74
  Turkey Couscous Salad 159
artichoke hearts
  Summer Vegetable Casserole 58
asparagus
  Risotto with Spring Vegetables 67
aubergines
  Ratatouille 138
  Roast Summer Vegetables 128
  Sweet & Sour Pasta 68
  Vegetarian Paella 113
avocados
  Chicken & Avocado Salad 162

bacon
  Bacon & Lentil Soup 46
  Beef Stew with Olives 104
  Boston Baked Beans 133
  Chicken & Avocado Salad 162
  Chicken with New Potatoes &
    Bacon 93
  Clams with Bacon & Breadcrumb
    Topping 24
  Neapolitan Beef 88
  Tagliatelle Bolognese 52
  Warm Bacon & Egg Salad 175
bamboo shoots
  Sweet & Sour Chicken Wings 19
beans
  Bean & Vegetable Soup 42
  Boston Baked Beans 133
  Gammon with Black-eyed Beans 54
  Pepper & Sweetcorn Salad 171

Pork & Beans 63
  Spring Vegetable Stew 121
  Summer Vegetable Casserole 58
  Sweetcorn & Butter Beans with Mixed
    Vegetables 157
  Tex-Mex Bean Dip 35
  Three Bean Chilli 82
  Vegetarian Paella 113
  Warm Chickpea Salad 40
beansprouts
  Vegetarian Spring Rolls 17
beef
  Beef Stew with Olives 104
  Caribbean Beef Stew 64
  Chinese Beef 117
  Goulash 55
  Neapolitan Beef 88
  Rich Beef & Coffee Stew 100
  Steak & Mozzarella Sandwiches 22
  Tagliatelle Bolognese 52
  Thick Beef & Baby Onion Casserole 109
  Traditional Pot Roast 70
beetroot
  Cajun Chicken Salad 165
berries
  Blackberry & Apple Loaf Cake 197
  New York Cheesecake with Fruit Sauce 192
Boston Cream Pie 193
bread
  Bread Rolls 147
  Cheese & Chive Bread 139
  Cheese & Ham Loaf 151
  Cornbread 172
  Country Loaf 180
broad beans
  Chicken Stew 108
  Risotto with Spring Vegetables 67
  Spicy Chicken with Sausage &
    Peppers 91
  Spring Vegetable Stew 121
  Summer Vegetable Casserole 58
broccoli
  Cheesy Broccoli Bake 166
Buttermilk Scones 176

Butterscotch Blondies 211

cabbage
   Braised Red Cabbage & Apples 145
   Chicken Braised with Red Cabbage 110
   Spring Vegetable Stew 121
   Stuffed Cabbage with Tomato Sauce 76
Caesar Salad with Garlic Croûtons 150
cakes & slices
   Almond Sponge Cake 196
   Blackberry & Apple Loaf Cake 197
   Boston Cream Pie 193
   Butterscotch Blondies 211
   Chocolate & Walnut Sponge Cake 208
   Cinnamon Swirl & Soured Cream Bundt
     Cake 186
   Double Fudge Brownies 187
   Madeira Cake with Orange Glaze 204
capers
   Maryland Crab Cakes 16
   Pork with Almonds 125
   Tuna Melts 34
carrots
   Bacon & Lentil Soup 46
   Bean & Vegetable Soup 42
   Beef Stew with Olives 104
   Carrot & Coriander Soup 32
   Chinese Beef 117
   Duck & Red Wine Stew 81
   Gammon with Black-eyed Beans 54
   Goulash 55
   Lamb Shanks with Olives 122
   Lentil & Vegetable Casserole 85
   Macaroni Salad 136
   Pork & Vegetable Ragout 118
   Risotto with Spring Vegetables 67
   Roast Vegetables 169
   Spring Vegetable Stew 121
   Tomato & Lentil Soup 30
   Traditional Pot Roast 70
   Vegetable Curry 71
   Vegetable Stew with Dumplings 78
   Vegetarian Spring Rolls 17
cauliflower
   Vegetable Curry 71

celery
   Bacon & Lentil Soup 46
   Bean & Vegetable Soup 42
   Duck & Red Wine Stew 81
   Gammon with Black-eyed Beans 54
   Macaroni Salad 136
   Oysters Rockefeller 36
   Potato & Egg Salad 168
   Stuffed Cabbage with Tomato Sauce 76
   Summer Vegetable Casserole 58
   Sweet & Sour Chicken Wings 19
   Tomato & Lentil Soup 30
   Vegetable Stew with Dumplings 78
   Waldorf Salad 154
cheese
   Caesar Salad with Garlic Croûtons 150
   Cheese & Chive Bread 139
   Cheese & Ham Loaf 151
   Cheesy Broccoli Bake 166
   Chicken & Avocado Salad 162
   Dauphinoise Potatoes 148
   Macaroni Cheese 142
   Mozzarella Cheese & Tomato Salad 130
   New York Cheesecake with Fruit Sauce 192
   Onion & Mozzarella Tartlets 27
   Rocket & Parmesan Salad with Pine
     Nuts 141
   Spinach & Herb Frittata 39
   Steak & Mozzarella Sandwiches 22
   Stuffed Cabbage with Tomato Sauce 76
   Tex-Mex Bean Dip 35
   Tuna Melts 34
   Warm Crab Dip 43
chicken
   BBQ Chicken Wings 45
   Cajun Chicken Salad 165
   Chicken & Avocado Salad 162
   Chicken & Mushroom Stew 84
   Chicken Braised with Red Cabbage 110
   Chicken Cacciatore 61
   Chicken in Mushroom & White Wine
     Sauce 101
   Chicken Satay Skewers with Peanut
     Sauce 49
   Chicken Stew 108
   Chicken with New Potatoes & Bacon 93

Chilli Chicken 124
Chipotle Chicken 73
Crispy Chicken Goujons with Honey &
    Mustard Dip 28
Easy Chinese Chicken 57
Nutty Chicken 99
Spicy Chicken with Sausage & Peppers 91
Sticky Ginger & Garlic Wings 38
Sweet & Sour Chicken Wings 19
chickpeas
    Caribbean Beef Stew 64
    Hummus with Crudités 23
    Warm Chickpea Salad 40
chillies, chilli sauce/powder
    Chilli Chicken 124
    Chipotle Chicken 73
    Deep-fried Chilli Corn Balls 31
    Pepper & Sweetcorn Salad 171
    Pork with Almonds 125
    Prawn Cocktail 14
    Spicy Chicken with Sausage &
        Peppers 91
    Sweet Potato Cakes 26
    Sweetcorn & Butter Beans with Mixed
        Vegetables 157
    Tex-Mex Bean Dip 35
    Three Bean Chilli 82
    Vegetable Curry 71
chocolate
    Boston Cream Pie 193
    Butterscotch Blondies 211
    Chocolate & Walnut Sponge Cake 208
    Chocolate Pots 198
    Double Fudge Brownies 187
Cinnamon Swirl & Soured Cream
    Bundt Cake 186
Clams with Bacon & Breadcrumb Topping 24
coconut
    Deep-fried Chilli Corn Balls 31
Country Loaf 180
courgettes
    Courgette Fritters 131
    Courgettes with Peppers & Tomatoes 103
    Lentil & Vegetable Casserole 85
    Ratatouille 138
    Roast Summer Vegetables 128
    Roast Vegetables 169

Sweet & Sour Pasta 68
Sweetcorn & Butter Beans with Mixed
    Vegetables 157
Turkey Couscous Salad 159
Vegetable Stew with Dumplings 78
couscous
    Turkey Couscous Salad 159
crabmeat
    Maryland Crab Cakes 16
    Warm Crab Dip 43
Crème Brûlée 195
Crêpes with Apples 210

desserts
    Apple Crumble 202
    Blushing Pears 213
    Chocolate Pots 198
    Crème Brûlée 195
    Crêpes with Apples 210
    Lemon Meringue Pie 207
    Magic Lemon Sponge Cake 191
    New York Cheesecake with Fruit Sauce 192
    Peach Cobbler 188
    Poached Peaches in Marsala Wine 201
    Rice Pudding 214
    Sweet Potato Pie 205
Duck & Red Wine Stew 81

eggs
    Baked Sweetcorn Puddings 163
    Chicken & Avocado Salad 162
    Crème Brûlée 195
    Lemon Meringue Pie 207
    Potato & Egg Salad 168
    Spinach & Herb Frittata 39
    Warm Bacon & Egg Salad 175

fennel
    Roast Summer Vegetables 128
    Rocket & Parmesan Salad with Pine
        Nuts 141
    Sea Bass with Fennel & Orange
        Juice 77
fish & seafood
    Clams with Bacon & Breadcrumb
        Topping 24
    Oysters Rockefeller 36

Sea Bass in Lemon Sauce 65
Sea Bass with Fennel & Orange Juice 77
Slow Cooker Salmon 96
Tuna Melts 34
see also crabmeat; prawns

gammon
　　Gammon Cooked in Cider 95
　　Gammon with Black-eyed Beans 54
ginger
　　Caribbean Beef Stew 64
　　Chicken Satay Skewers with Peanut
　　　Sauce 49
　　Chinese Beef 117
　　Easy Chinese Chicken 57
　　Sticky Ginger Garlic Wings 38
　　Vegetable Curry 71
　　Vegetarian Spring Rolls 17
Goulash 55
grapes
　　Waldorf Salad 154
green beans
　　Green Bean Casserole 153
　　Risotto with Spring Vegetables 67
　　Sweetcorn & Butter Beans with Mixed
　　　Vegetables 157
　　Vegetarian Paella 113

ham
　　Cheese & Ham Loaf 151
horseradish
　　Prawn Cocktail 14
Hummus with Crudités 23

juniper berries
　　Beef Stew with Olives 104
　　Chicken Braised with Red
　　　Cabbage 110
　　Gammon Cooked in Cider 95
　　Venison Casserole 60

lamb
　　Lamb & Rice Soup 20
　　Lamb Shanks with Olives 122
　　Lamb Stew with Red Peppers 107
leeks
　　Lentil & Vegetable Casserole 85
　　Pork & Vegetable Ragout 118
　　Summer Vegetable Casserole 58

lemons
　　Lemon Meringue Pie 207
　　Magic Lemon Sponge Cake 191
　　New York Cheesecake with Fruit
　　　Sauce 192
　　Sea Bass in Lemon Sauce 65
lentils
　　Bacon & Lentil Soup 46
　　Lentil & Vegetable Casserole 85
　　Tomato & Lentil Soup 30

Madeira Cake with Orange Glaze 204
mangoes
　　Cajun Chicken Salad 165
mushrooms
　　Chicken & Mushroom Stew 84
　　Chicken in Mushroom & White
　　　Wine Sauce 101
　　Chinese Beef 117
　　Sea Bass in Lemon Sauce 65
　　Vegetarian Paella 113
　　Vegetarian Spring Rolls 17

noodles
　　Chinese Beef 117
　　Vegetarian Spring Rolls 17
nuts
　　Butterscotch Blondies 211
　　Chicken Braised with Red Cabbage 110
　　Chicken Satay Skewers with Peanut
　　　Sauce 49
　　Stuffed Cabbage with Tomato Sauce 76
　　see also almonds; walnuts

oats
　　Apple Crumble 202
okra
　　Pork & Vegetable Ragout 118
olives
　　Beef Stew with Olives 104
　　Lamb Shanks with Olives 122
　　Pork with Almonds 125
　　Sweet & Sour Pasta 68
　　Warm Chickpea Salad 40
oranges
　　Baked Acorn Squash 144
　　Lamb Stew with Red Peppers 107
　　Madeira Cake with Orange Glaze 204
　　New York Cheesecake with Fruit Sauce 192
　　Sea Bass with Fennel & Orange Juice 77
　　Thick Beef & Baby Onion Casserole 109
Oysters Rockefeller 36

pasta
    Fettuccini with Prawn & Tomato
      Sauce 114
    Macaroni Cheese 142
    Macaroni Salad 136
    Sweet & Sour Pasta 68
    Tagliatelle Bolognese 52
peaches
    Peach Cobbler 188
    Poached Peaches in Marsala Wine 201
pears
    Blushing Pears 213
peas
    Duck & Red Wine Stew 81
    Risotto with Spring Vegetables 67
    Vegetable Curry 71
peppers
    Caribbean Beef Stew 64
    Chicken Stew 108
    Clams with Bacon & Breadcrumb
      Topping 24
    Courgettes with Peppers & Tomatoes 103
    Gammon with Black-eyed Beans 54
    Jalapeño Pork Chops 92
    Lamb Stew with Red Peppers 107
    Lentil & Vegetable Casserole 85
    Macaroni Salad 136
    Onion & Mozzarella Tartlets 27
    Pepper & Sweetcorn Salad 171
    Pork with Peppers & Apricots 74
    Ratatouille 138
    Roast Pepper Salad 156
    Roast Summer Vegetables 128
    Roast Vegetables 169
    Spicy Chicken with Sausage & Peppers 91
    Steak & Mozzarella Sandwiches 22
    Summer Vegetable Casserole 58
    Sweet & Sour Chicken Wings 19
    Sweet & Sour Pasta 68
    Sweetcorn & Butter Beans with Mixed
      Vegetables 157
    Three Bean Chilli 82
    Vegetarian Paella 113
pine nuts
    Rocket & Parmesan Salad with Pine
      Nuts 141
    Turkey Couscous Salad 159
pineapple
    Jalapeño Pork Chops 92
    Sweet & Sour Chicken Wings 19
polenta
    Cornbread 172
    Deep-fried Chilli Corn Balls 31
    Polenta Balls 160
Polenta Balls 160

pork
    Jalapeño Pork Chops 92
    Pork & Beans 63
    Pork & Vegetable Ragout 118
    Pork with Almonds 125
    Pork with Apple & Herbs 87
    Pork with Peppers & Apricots 74
potatoes
    Bean & Vegetable Soup 42
    Chicken with New Potatoes &
      Bacon 93
    Dauphinoise Potatoes 148
    Garlic & Herb Potato Wedges 183
    Lentil & Vegetable Casserole 85
    Perfect Mashed Potatoes 135
    Pork & Beans 63
    Potato & Egg Salad 168
    Roast Red Potato Salad 178
    Roast Vegetables 169
    Spring Vegetable Stew 121
    Traditional Pot Roast 70
    Vegetable Stew with Dumplings 78
prawns
    Fettuccini with Prawn & Tomato
      Sauce 114
    Prawn Cocktail 14

radishes
    Cajun Chicken Salad 165
Ratatouille 138
rice
    Lamb & Rice Soup 20
    Rice Pudding 214
    Risotto with Spring Vegetables 67
    Vegetarian Paella 113
rocket
    Rocket & Parmesan Salad with
      Pine Nuts 141
    Spicy Chicken with Sausage & Peppers 91

salads
    Caesar Salad with Garlic Croûtons 150
    Cajun Chicken Salad 165
    Chicken & Avocado Salad 162
    Macaroni Salad 136
    Mozzarella Cheese & Tomato
      Salad 130
    Pepper & Sweetcorn Salad 171
    Potato & Egg Salad 168

Roast Pepper Salad 156
Roast Vegetables 169
Rocket & Parmesan Salad with Pine
    Nuts 141
Turkey Couscous Salad 159
Waldorf Salad 154
Warm Bacon & Egg Salad 175
Warm Chickpea Salad 40
sausages
    Gammon with Black-eyed Beans 54
    Spicy Chicken with Sausage & Peppers 91
sea bass
    Sea Bass in Lemon Sauce 65
    Sea Bass with Fennel & Orange Juice 77
soups
    Bacon & Lentil Soup 46
    Bean & Vegetable Soup 42
    Carrot & Coriander Soup 32
    Lamb & Rice Soup 20
    Tomato & Lentil Soup 30
spinach
    Creamed Spinach 134
    Oysters Rockefeller 36
    Slow Cooker Salmon 96
    Spicy Chicken with Sausage & Peppers 91
    Spinach & Herb Frittata 39
squash
    Baked Acorn Squash 144
    Caribbean Beef Stew 64
    Pork & Vegetable Ragout 118
    Vegetable Stew with Dumplings 78
Summer Vegetable Casserole 58
sweet potatoes
    Sweet Potato Cakes 26
    Sweet Potato Pie 205
sweetcorn
    Baked Sweetcorn Puddings 163
    Chicken Stew 108
    Deep-fried Chilli Corn Balls 31
    Pepper & Sweetcorn Salad 171
    Spring Vegetable Stew 121
    Sweetcorn & Butter Beans with Mixed
        Vegetables 157
    Vegetable Stew with Dumplings 78

tomatoes
    Bean & Vegetable Soup 42
    Caribbean Beef Stew 64
    Chicken & Avocado Salad 162
    Chicken & Mushroom Stew 84

Chicken Cacciatore 61
Chicken Stew 108
Chipotle Chicken 73
Courgettes with Peppers & Tomatoes 103
Fettuccini with Prawn & Tomato
    Sauce 114
Goulash 55
Lamb Shanks with Olives 122
Lamb Stew with Red Peppers 107
Mozzarella Cheese & Tomato Salad 130
Neapolitan Beef 88
Onion & Mozzarella Tartlets 27
Pork & Beans 63
Pork & Vegetable Ragout 118
Pork with Almonds 125
Ratatouille 138
Roast Pepper Salad 156
Roast Summer Vegetables 128
Stuffed Cabbage with Tomato
    Sauce 76
Sweet & Sour Pasta 68
Sweetcorn & Butter Beans with Mixed
    Vegetables 157
Tagliatelle Bolognese 52
Tomato & Lentil Soup 30
Vegetable Curry 71
Vegetarian Paella 113
Warm Bacon & Egg Salad 175
Traditional Pot Roast 70
Tuna Melts 34
Turkey Couscous Salad 159
turnips
    Bacon & Lentil Soup 46
    Summer Vegetable Casserole 58

Venison Casserole 60

Waldorf Salad 154
walnuts
    Cajun Chicken Salad 165
    Chocolate & Walnut Sponge Cake 208
    Cinnamon Swirl & Soured Cream Bundt
        Cake 186
    Double Fudge Brownies 187
    Nutty Chicken 99

yams
    Glazed Yams 181
Yorkshire Puddings 25

Happy Cooking
from

Blueberry
Hill